SHAKESPEARE'S STORIES
Histories

Retold by Beverley Birch

Illustrated by Robina Green

PETER BEDRICK BOOKS
NEW YORK

First American edition published in 1988 by
Peter Bedrick Books, New York

Text copyright © 1988 Beverley Birch
Illustrations copyright © Macdonald & Co. (Publishers) Ltd.
All rights reserved.

Published by agreement with Macdonald & Co. (Publishers) Ltd., London.
A member of Pergamon MCC Publishing Corporation plc.

Library of Congress Cataloging-in-Publication Data
Birch, Beverley.
    Shakespeare's stories: histories/retold by Beverley Birch;
illustrated by Robina Green.
       p. cm.
    Summary: Presents the stories of five of Shakespeare's plays:
Antony and Cleopatra, Richard III, Henry IV, Henry V, and Julius Caesar.
    ISBN 0–87226–192–1
    1. Shakespeare, William, 1564–1616 – Adaptations – Juvenile
literature. 2. Shakespeare, William, 1564–1616 – Histories – Juvenile
literature. [1. Shakespeare, William, 1564–1616 – Adaptations.]
    I. Green, Robina, ill. II. Shakespeare, William, 1564–1616. Plays.
Selections. 1988. III. Title.
    PR2877.B45 1988   88–15693
                                                               CIP
                                                                AC

Printed in Great Britain
10 9 8 7 6 5 4 3 2 1

Series Editor: Luigi Bonomi
Series Design: Sylvia Kwan
Production: Rosemary Bishop

The author's grateful thanks are due to Priscilla Stone for her perceptive
comment, criticism and never-flagging encouragement, and to Ruairidh
and Calum MacLean, who have tirelessly read the scripts with the
healthy scepticism of a young eye, and whose comments have been a
source of inspiration and much-valued guidance.

-CONTENTS-

Henry the Fourth

King Henry IV was on the throne of England and little more than three restless years had passed since he, as Henry Bolingbroke, had returned hot-foot from banishment in France. His aim, he had declared, was to reclaim his inheritance as Duke of Lancaster, for had not England's extravagant young king, Richard II, seized all on Henry's father's death, lands, property and revenue, to pay for wars in Ireland?

But, with the swelling power of the northern lords of England, young Henry Bolingbroke had done much more. He had pushed his cousin Richard from the throne and seized the crown himself.

It did not sit easy on King Henry's head. He had taken it, he said, to right the wrongs of England under Richard, for Richard had been king since he was a child and he was careless with the privileges of power, casual with its duties and responsibilities. But Henry never could forget that Richard was the rightful and anointed king, the seventh generation of a golden line of England's kings stretching back across more than two hundred years. And Henry was haunted by the memory of Richard, deposed, imprisoned and murdered in his cell. It loomed always to remind him that Richard's blood still stained his hands, that he had usurped the crown and by that deed had opened the viciousness of civil war to England.

The rivalry between those loyal to dead Richard, and those loyal to live Henry had bruised and torn the kingdom since that time, sons fighting fathers, cousins, brothers, daubing England's soil with her people's blood, so that King Henry had grown heavy with his guilt and longed to bring peace to the land. He longed also to show some atonement for his crime by journeying to Jerusalem to fight for Christ . . .

But it was not to be, in this troubled, stormy year of 1402. From west and north, the messengers came galloping to the king at Westminster with news that made his burdens heavier. In Wales, there was an uprising led by the powerful Welsh lord, Owen Glendower: in the latest battle a thousand Englishmen had joined the multitudes of slain. And in Northumberland a Scottish invasion led by the formidable Earl of Douglas had been met by the men of Northumberland under the command of the spirited son of the Earl of Northumberland, Harry Percy.

But the news from Northumberland was better than the news from Wales. The long and bloody battle had been won by Harry Percy and many Scottish earls taken prisoner. It was a conquest for a prince to boast of!

Yet in that thought lay greater sorrow for the king: why should the Lord Northumberland be father to so valiant and so honourable a son as Harry Percy, while he, the King of England saw only riot and dishonour stain the brow of his son, Harry, Prince of Wales, the good-for nothing, idle heir to the English throne. His stamping ground was no bloody battlefield of honour but the teeming streets and steaming drunken taverns of London.

The king sighed heavily, 'Oh that it could be proved that some night-tripping fairy had exchanged our children! Then would I have his Harry and he mine . . .' He shook the thought away with difficulty. There was more urgent business to be dealt with: honourable and valiant though he was, young Harry Percy was also far too bold and proud for comfort. He had refused to hand over to the king the prisoners taken in the battle with the Scots; their ransoms should have swelled the royal coffers, but young Hotspur, as Harry Percy was more often called, wished to keep them for himself.

'He sends me word,' said Henry, frowning, 'that I shall have none but Mordake, Earl of Fife!'

'This is his uncle's teaching: this is Worcester's doing,' the king's advisers told him. 'He is malevolent to you in all aspects, which makes him bristle up young Hotspur against your dignity.'

'I have sent for him to answer this,' said Henry, and brooded on the prospect. He sensed the rumblings of a discord greater than any quarrel about Scottish prisoners. The Percies, the family of the Earl of Northumberland and his brother, the Earl of Worcester, were the wealthy northern lords whose armed powers had lifted Henry to the throne and toppled Richard. Ambition, always strong in them, was swelling restlessly, and it seemed to Henry that their demands upon him for his debt to them were growing far beyond control.

Across the years he heard the echo of the fallen Richard's voice. 'Northumberland,' he had said, as that lord led him off to prison, 'Northumberland, you ladder by which my cousin Bolingbroke ascends my throne, the time shall come when foul sin, gathering head, shall break into corruption: you will think, though he divide the realm and give you half, it is too little, helping him to all. And he shall think that you, who know how to plant unrightful kings, will know again another way to pluck him headlong from the usurped throne . . .'

While the king was contemplating how diseases grew so dangerously within the kingdom's heart, his son Harry, Prince of Wales, was neither troubled now, nor had he ever been with the weight of serious matters such as these. The only weight that occupied his thoughts was the vast mountain of a man spreadeagled on a couch, from whom the snores rose and fell like the rumblings of a deep cavern underground.

The prince looked down at him, a half-smile flickering across his face. Then he prodded the mountain, somewhere in its shuddering peak. The rumblings turned to a whistling, the mountain rolled a little, mumbled, twitched, and sank back into the whistling roar . . .

The prince prodded again. The mountain groaned. In the eastern regions a plump pink face appeared, a single eye that blinked and closed again, then thought better of it, and two pink eyes opened blearily upon the afternoon.

'Now Hal,' the mountain said, and heaved itself up to become the portly shape of Sir John Falstaff, 'what time of day is it, lad?'

For answer Hal grinned broadly. 'You are so fat-witted with drinking of wine and sleeping upon benches after noon!' he exclaimed. 'What a devil have you to do with the time of day? Unless hours were cups of wine and minutes capons . . .'

'Indeed,' the old knight chuckled, rising like a whale from the couch and making his way yawning to the table in search of drink to fuel him after the laborious task of his interrupted slumbers, 'we that take purses go by the moon . . .' He sank thankfully to a seat, and drained a cup of wine. Then a most important thought popped to his brain. 'Now, sweet Hal, when you are king, let not us that are squires of the night's body be

9

called thieves of the day's beauty: let us be . . .' he searched for some
choice phrase of adequate dignity, 'let us be "gentlemen of the shade",
"minions of the moon"' he pronounced the words roundly, 'and let men
say we are men of good government, being governed, as the sea is, by
our noble mistress the moon, under whose gaze we steal . . .'

'You say well,' applauded the prince, 'for the fortune of us that are
the moon's men ebbs and flows like the sea, being governed, as the sea
is, by the moon. A purse of gold most resolutely snatched on Monday
night and most dissolutely spent on Tuesday morning, now is in as low
an ebb as the foot of the ladder, and by and by as high a flow as the ridge
of the hangman's gallows!'

Mention of the gallows, the fate of many a thief, made jovial Sir John
Falstaff shift uneasily. He looked at Hal reproachfully for so clouding
the jesting of a moment with such gloomy matters. 'Shall there be
gallows standing in England when you are king?' he wondered. 'Do not
you, when you are king, hang a thief.'

'No,' Hal assured him solemnly, 'you shall.'

'Shall I?' Falstaff contemplated this intriguing prospect with
wonderment and peered across his cup at the merry mocking eyes of the
young prince. Then he sighed, and took on a look of pained endurance,
'You are indeed able to corrupt a saint,' he complained, with an upward
look towards the heavens. 'You have done much harm upon me, Hal;
God forgive you for it! Before I knew you, Hal, I knew nothing; and
now am I little better than one of the wicked. I must give over this life,'
he intoned piously, 'and will give it over. By the Lord, if I do not, I am
a villain,' and he closed his eyes as if in prayer, but was unable to
maintain this stance for long, bowled over as he was by the enthusiastic
entrance of Poins, a young friend of the prince, with news of a new
escapade afoot: a robbery.

'My lads, my lads,' Poins cried, with glee, 'tomorrow morning, at
four o'clock, early at Gadshill there are pilgrims going to Canterbury
with rich offerings and traders riding from London with fat purses: I
have masks for you all, you have horses for yourselves. We may do it as
secure as sleep. If you will go, I will stuff your purses full of crowns; if
you will not, stay at home and be hanged!'

Falstaff chortled, the churchlike chant of atonement instantly
abandoned for this better sport. 'Hal, will you make one of us?' he
cried.

'Who, I rob? I a thief? not I,' the prince protested.

'There's neither honesty, manhood, nor good fellowship in you,' grumbled Falstaff, for whom the jaunt would be a good deal less jolly for the absence of the prince. 'By the Lord,' he sulked, 'I'll be a traitor then, when you are king,' but he nevertheless allowed his great bulk to be heaved from the room, on the promise that Poins would find a way to knock the prince from this path of unlooked-for honesty.

Poins did have a way, though it was not as Falstaff might have guessed. He had a joke afoot, for which he needed Prince Hal's help. It was this: Falstaff and his three companions would rob the pilgrims; Poins and Hal, disguised, would then rob Falstaff and his friends, and the joke would be in the incomprehensible lies which the old rogue would tell afterwards, of how thirty men, at least, he fought with, what blows and wounds were suffered . . .

Prince Hal laughed: without doubt the incorrigible old villain would gild the story of the skirmish as though it was the epic of a war! 'Well, I'll go with you,' he declared, and off went Poins to make arrangements for their escapade.

The prince's rooms were, for the first time, silent. For a long moment he sat there plunged in thought. How well he knew them all, these companions of his prank-filled days: Poins, Falstaff, and the raucous motley of souls who joined the old knight's boisterous misdeeds or floated with him through his days of gadding humour. And he, the Prince of Wales, was one of them.

Hal contemplated this fact soberly, for he knew what charges were laid against him daily at his father's Court, how tarnished and twisted was his reputation and how bitterly his father spoke of him. He knew that, for a while, he would still be one of them.

Yet he knew too that there would come a time when this must end. There would come an hour when the future King of England must shake off his idle youth, and with it shake away the friends . . .

He pushed the thought away and stared beyond, into the future. For how much brighter would he shine, emerging from the smothering mists of all his misdemeanours into the sunshine of his royalty, transformed before the country's watching eyes from shallow youth into the rounded golden fullness of a king!

Across the council chamber in the palace, King Henry eyed the Percies grimly: the Earl of Northumberland with his brother, Earl of Worcester, and his son, Hotspur. He could see in Worcester's smouldering eye a world of scarce-hidden resentments that the Percies who had helped the king to greatness should be hauled before the council to explain their deeds.

'Worcester, go,' the king commanded, 'for I do see danger and disobedience in your eye. When we need your use and counsel, we shall send for you.'

Without a word the Earl of Worcester left, leaving his brother and his nephew to argue with the king upon the matter of the Scottish prisoners.

Hotspur was warrior enough to argue for them all. 'My liege,' he protested energetically, 'I did deny no prisoners!' It was, he claimed, a mere mistake. 'I remember, when the fight was done, when I was dry with rage, breathless and faint, leaning upon my sword, there came a certain lord, neat and trimly dressed, fresh as a bridegroom, who, as the soldiers bore dead bodies by, called them untaught knaves, unmannerly, to bring a slovenly and unhandsome corpse between the wind and his nobility!'

The scene painted so vividly by the hero of the hour drew smiles and nods of sympathy from all around the council chamber. Who could blame a Hotspur, cold and aching with his battle-wounds for losing patience with a popinjay! He had answered angrily to the pretty, perfumed lord's demands, amongst which there must have been the king's request for prisoners, but under such circumstances, and after such a conquest for the crown, this misdemeanour was surely slight and could not be held against the valiant young man!

'Why yet,' the king broke in, 'Why yet he does withhold his prisoners.'

Silence fell around the room. There was no answer to this charge, for it was true. And there was more: Hotspur also gave conditions to the king! He demanded that Henry should pay the ransom for Hotspur's brother-in-law, Lord Edmund Mortimer, the Earl of March, who had been captured by the fiery Welshman, Glendower. But Mortimer had led a thousand Englishmen to die against the Welsh, and then had married Glendower's daughter! It was an act of treachery beyond

redemption in Henry's eyes, to join thus with the rebellious, wild Welsh lord.

'Shall our coffers then, be emptied to redeem a traitor home?' he demanded grimly. 'Shall we buy treason? No, on the barren mountain let him starve, for I shall never hold that man my friend whose tongue shall ask me for one penny cost to ransom home revolted Mortimer!'

'Revolted Mortimer!' yelled Hotspur, incensed beyond all measure at the accusation.

Before the storm of Hotspur's anger, the king's rage became the coldness of hard steel.

'Henceforth let me not hear you speak of Mortimer!' he said, with icy menace. 'Send us your prisoners, or you will hear of it!' And on this note the king swept from the council chamber, the lords all moving silently in his wake, to leave only Hotspur and his father in the room.

Hotspur glared after the departing king. 'If the devil come and roar for them, I will not send them!' he burst out, and rushed to follow the king and tell him so.

'What, drunk with anger?' said his father, catching hold of him, for Worcester was coming back, and it was clear to Northumberland that the three of them had much to talk about, and fast. In this dark world of rivalries which bred the stench of blood and civil strife, the senses of men like Northumberland and Worcester had been sharpened to sniff the shifting currents of the winds of power, and the prevailing wind that blew towards them now was a cold one, deathly cold . . .

Fierce Hotspur's fury, though, was burn enough to warm them. 'Speak of Mortimer,' he yelled, pacing to and fro. 'I will speak of him, and I will join with him: for him I will empty all these veins drop by drop in the dust, I will lift down-trod Mortimer as high in the air as this unthankful king, as this ungrateful and cankered Bolingbroke!'

Furiously he greeted his returning uncle, 'When I urged the ransom of my wife's brother, then his cheek looked pale and on my face he turned an eye of death, trembling even at the name of Mortimer!'

'I cannot blame him,' Worcester said, carefully. 'Was he not proclaimed by Richard that is dead as heir to the crown?'

Hotspur stopped, and swung to look at them. Worcester looked at Northumberland, and Northumberland looked back at Worcester. The time, it seemed, had come when they must speak to this young hot-head of the north of matters brewing, affairs of utmost secrecy and urgency . . .

14

It was easier said than done. At each word the impatient warrior charged off again to do in words, here in the council chamber, what the battlefield would shortly draw from him against the king, 'By heaven,' he cried, 'it would be an easy leap to pluck bright honour from the pale-faced moon, or dive into the bottom of the deep and pluck up drowned honour by the locks!'

'Hear you, cousin, a word,' Worcester interrupted wearily.

Hotspur heard nothing. 'All studies here I solemnly defy,' he vowed, 'save how to gall and pinch this Bolingbroke and that same swashbuckling Prince of Wales!'

They calmed him, in the end, long enough, at least, to reveal their plans: first, Hotspur to go to his Scottish prisoners. They must be returned, without demanding ransom, to the Earl of Douglas, for by this gesture they would buy the certain support of Scotland for their venture. Next, his father to go to their kinsman, the Archbishop of York, who was already drawing up the foundations of rebellion against the king . . .

'I smell it: upon my life, it will do well,' breathed Hotspur, understanding suddenly. 'And then the power of Scotland and the power of York to join with Mortimer!'

'When time is ripe, which will be suddenly,' Worcester murmured, 'I'll steal to Glendower and Lord Mortimer, where you and the Earl of Douglas and our powers shall meet . . .'

'Uncle, farewell,' Hotspur clasped his hand. 'Oh, let the hours be short till fields and blows and groans applaud our sport!'

Rustling darkness on the highway near Gadshill; four o'clock on a chill, dank morning; whisperings and heavy stumblings amid cracking twigs. An enormous flapping figure loomed up against the sky like some gigantic wounded bat.

The bat had the plump, puffing face of Falstaff. It peered from beneath a cavernous hood, his nose no longer pink with drink but red with cold and his eyes rolling with the eternal struggle to stay upright against all odds.

'Poins! Hal!' he hissed into the blackness. 'A plague upon you both! I'll starve before I'll rob a foot further.' He staggered, whirling like a spinning top to keep his balance. 'Eight yards of uneven ground is threescore and ten miles afoot with me, and the stony-hearted villains know it well enough,' he moaned. 'A plague upon it when villains cannot be true to one another! Give me my horse, you rogues . . .'

'Peace, you fat-guts,' came the voice of Hal, and a shadow melted and reformed to make the prince's crouching shape. 'Lie down! Lay your ear close to the ground and listen if you can hear the tread of travellers.'

'Have you any levers to lift me up again, being down,' grumbled the fat knight. 'Good Prince Hal, help me to my horse, good king's son,' he pleaded.

'Out, you rogue!' said Hal, thoroughly enjoying this merciless torture of the old vagabond, 'shall I be the keeper of your horse?'

'Go hang yourself in your own heir-apparent garters,' snarled Falstaff, floundering across the stony ground like a beached whale. More bushy shadows melted and became the shapes of his three fellow robbers.

'On with your masks,' came the hasty cry, for victims could be heard approaching in the narrow lane.

'How many be there of them?'

'Some eight or ten.'

''Zounds, will they not rob us?' muttered Falstaff in alarm.

The travellers were very close, voices raised against the menace of the dark. There came a sudden yell, scufflings and several blows, and a moment later found the hapless travellers bound in a bundle on the ground and bereft of all their money, which Falstaff and his fellow robbers bore triumphantly away, with Hal and Poins nowhere to be seen.

After a short while, Prince Hal and Poins moved silently across the lane behind the fat knight and his exultant friends.

'Your money!' demanded the prince in ringing tones.

'Villains,' bellowed Poins for good measure, and both together set upon the startled band, who thereupon let out a shriek of terror and took to their heels, though the fat knight aimed several blows at them before joining the general retreat.

Doubled up with laughter at the ease with which the would-be thieves had been transformed into bellowing victims, the prince and Poins listened to the crash and moan of Falstaff lurching through the undergrowth.

'How the old rogue roared!' Poins almost wept with glee to think of

all the lies he would produce to excuse the loss of their ill-gotten gains . . .

Hotspur was pacing angrily again. He had received a letter from a gentleman whose support he'd hoped for in the rebellion against the king. The reply was a quite unexpected 'no'. 'The purpose you undertake is dangerous, the friends you have named uncertain,' the gentleman had written.

Impatiently Hotspur flung the letter down. 'What a frosty-spirited rogue is this,' he cried, 'Why, my lord of York commends the plot! Is there not my father, my uncle and myself, Lord Edmund Mortimer, my lord of York and Owen Glendower? Is there not, besides, the Earl of Douglas? Have I not all their letters to meet me in arms by the ninth of next month, and are not some of them set out already?' And in that instant he made up his mind to start that very night for Wales.

'How now, Kate,' he greeted his pretty wife, but evaded her searching eyes. He knew she had seen the grim preoccupation of his

17

thoughts and was becoming anxious. 'I must leave you within these two hours,' he told her.

'What is it carries you away?' she pleaded.

'Why, my horse, my love, my horse,' he smiled, and tried to move away.

'Out, you mad-headed ape!' she exclaimed, half in frustrated anger, half in laughter, 'In faith, I'll know your business, Harry, that I will. I fear my brother Mortimer has sent for you . . .'

He would not tell her, though. She tried anger, threats, loving pleas, but all to no avail. She could not, he told her, give away a secret if she did not know it, and their enterprise against the king was of the utmost secrecy and danger.

'But hark you, Kate,' he said, 'where I go, there shall you go too; today I will set forth, tomorrow you,' and this bare comfort was all that she could eke from him.

While this hot-headed, valiant Harry of the north was busy in Northumberland with preparations for his war against the king, in London, in the noisy revelry of the Boar's Head Tavern in Eastcheap, the tarnished Harry of the south awaited the doughty robbers of Gadshill and spent his time contemplating the motley souls who gathered in that inn. What a ragged course he steered among them, friend to all, the king of courtesy! 'I am not yet of Percy's mind, the Hotspur of the north,' he assured Poins, 'he that kills some six or seven Scots at breakfast, washes his hands, and says to his wife, "Fie upon this quiet life! I want work." "Oh my sweet Harry," says she, "how many have you killed today?" "Some fourteen," he answers, "a trifle, a trifle . . ."'

But this boisterous mockery of the northern prince of honour was interrupted by the clatter of Falstaff and his fellow thieves returning, puffed and sweating with their flight and bursting to tell the horror of their escapade. The prince and Poins exchanged expectant looks, and waited.

It was worth the wait. 'There be four of us have taken a thousand pound this day morning,' Falstaff announced importantly.

'Where is it, Jack, where is it?' urged the prince keeping as much of a straight face as he could manage.

'Where is it! Taken from us it is: a hundred upon poor four of us!'

Falstaff mopped his sweating brow and rolled his eyes in horror at the memory.

'What, a hundred, man?' whistled the prince, scarcely able to contain his glee at the sheer size of this monstrous lie.

'I am a rogue if I were not fighting with a dozen of them two hours together!' declared the old villain, and without so much as a single blush he proceeded to describe the quantities of sword-cuts through his clothing, on his chest, his leg, 'I have escaped by a miracle! If I did not fight with fifty of them, I am a bunch of radish,' he declared, his nose, in the excitement of the tale becoming more and more like that glorious-coloured vegetable.

'Pray God you have not murdered some of them,' the prince said solemnly.

This was further cue for a most exotic multiplication of numbers. 'I have peppered two of them, two rogues in buckram suits,' Falstaff assured him, 'I tell you what, Hal, if I tell a lie, spit in my face, call me a horse . . . . Four rogues in buckram let drive at me, I made no more ado but took all their seven points . . .'

'Seven,' gasped the prince. 'Why, there were but four even now.'

'Seven, by these hilts, or I am a villain,' Falstaff assured him, unabashed. 'But I followed close, and with a thought seven of the eleven . . .'

'Oh, monstrous! Eleven buckram men grown out of two,' gasped Hal, unable to contain his merriment any longer. 'These lies are like their father, gross as a mountain! Why you clay-brained guts, you knotty-pated fool. We *two*,' he indicated Poins and himself, 'we *two* saw you four set on four and bind them, and were masters of their wealth. See now how a plain tale shall put you down,' he wagged a warning finger. 'Then did we *two* set on you four! Falstaff, you carried your guts away as nimbly, and roared for mercy as ever I heard a bull-calf . . .'

Falstaff, on the point of launching into the full epic narrative of how he'd soundly trounced an army single-handed, stopped, open-mouthed and in mid-breath. His eyes swivelled from side to side, measuring the enormity of what had just been said. He blinked. He licked his lips. He hitched his clothing straight and sat a little taller on the chair. 'By the Lord,' he said suddenly, with an air of unfailing wisdom, 'I knew you as well as he that made you! Why hear you, my masters,' he appealed to his audience, the picture of honest innocence, 'was it for me to kill the heir-apparent? Should I turn upon the true prince? The lion will not touch the true prince!'

He peered then into Hal's face. He chuckled, he chortled, then he guffawed and slapped his enormous knee with a crack like thunder. 'But by the Lord, lads, I am glad you have the money! Gallants, lads, boys, hearts of gold, shall we be merry? Shall we have a play?'

'And the plot shall be your running away,' yelled Hal, truth, lies and all disappearing beneath the vastness of the old rogue's humour.

But there came an unwelcome intrusion on their merriment: a solemn gentleman from the royal Court who brought a summons from king to prince. Falstaff obligingly went off to send the fellow packing, but returned with uneasy news: Hotspur, Northumberland, Worcester, Glendower, Mortimer, Douglas, were all in arms against the king. 'Your father's beard has turned white with the news, and you may buy land now as cheap as stinking mackerel,' Falstaff informed Hal. 'Well,' he said, contemplating his young friend soberly, 'You will be horribly scolded tomorrow when you come to your father; practice an answer.'

Hal returned the sober stare soberly. Then a flash of laughter lit up his face again. 'You stand for my father, and examine me upon the particulars of my life.'

Falstaff was transfixed by the sheer audacity and pure delight of such a scheme, 'Shall I?' he squealed, and without further ado settled himself in state upon a chair, a dagger held right royally as the monarch's sceptre and his bald head crowned with the glory of a wine-spattered tassled cushion. 'Give me a cup of wine to make my eyes look red, that it may be thought I have wept!' he commanded, and turned a frowning countenance upon the tittering onlookers who drew near to watch the fun.

Then regally he turned a doleful eye upon Prince Hal, who stood in the manner of a scolded child before the gigantic wine-red 'king'. Sorrowfully he reproached the erring prince for the wildness of his ways and the wickedness of his disreputable companions. 'And yet,' he nodded solemnly, 'there is a virtuous man whom I have often noted in your company . . . a good portly man, of a cheerful look, a pleasing eye and a most noble carriage; and now I remember,' he raised his voice above the hiccuping guffaws which greeted this pantomime, 'his name is Falstaff. Harry, I see virtue in his looks. There is virtue in that Falstaff: him keep with you, the rest banish!'

'Do you speak like a king?' exclaimed Hal, unexpectedly nettled by this mockery of his father. 'You stand for me, and I'll play my father.'

'Depose me?' frowned Falstaff to hoots of laughter, but resigned his cushion happily enough, and stood in mock trembling fear to receive the wrath of the new 'king'.

'There is a devil haunts you,' Hal intoned, with studied solemnity and a coldly glittering eye not unlike his father's, 'a devil in the likeness of an old fat man . . . Why do you converse with that swollen parcel of dropsies, that huge bombard of wine, that roasted ox with the pudding in his belly, that father ruffian . . .' he went on above the shrieks of laughter that met this return thrust of the contest. 'What is he good for, but to taste wine and drink it, to carve a chicken and eat it?'

'Whom means your grace?' whimpered Falstaff in mock terror.

'That villainous, abominable misleader of youth, Falstaff, that old white-bearded Satan,' mercilessly Prince Hal pressed the attack home.

And beneath the laughter Falstaff was, to tell the truth, more uneasy than he would have liked it seen. There was a cold edge to the prince's words he did not like to hear, not in the things he said, which were meat and drink to the old knight's persistent jollity, but in the underlying thread of hardness in the tone. There was in that the threat of things to come . . .

'If to be old and merry is a sin,' Falstaff protested roundly to cover his discomfort, 'then many an old host that I know is damned. Banish all,' he urged the prince, 'but for sweet Jack Falstaff, kind Jack Falstaff, true Jack Falstaff, valiant Jack Falstaff, banish not him from Harry's company: banish plump Jack and banish all the world!'

'I do,' Prince Hal replied, 'I will.'

There was a silence, too long and too complete, in which errant prince stared at the companion of his erring ways, and the old knight felt suddenly cold, as though a door was shutting, and he caught on the wrong side of it, for though words bounced off the old fellow's plump jollity, the sudden thought of separation from his merry prince, iced him to his bones. Then the moment was broken by a loud knocking at the door: the sheriff looking for the band of robbers from Gadshill, and one particularly well-known, a gross fat man . . .

Swiftly, all else but friendship forgotten now, Falstaff was pushed into hiding by the prince. 'The man, I do assure you, is not here,' lied the Prince of Wales to the sheriff, and that stern gentleman of the law reluctantly withdrew, forced to accept his word.

Behind a curtain, Falstaff was fast asleep and snoring loudly after the energetic revelry of this busy day. Hal stood looking down at him and sighed. In the morning he must answer his father's summons to appear at the Court, and they were all now for the wars . . .

In Glendower's Welsh stronghold, far from the reach of King Henry's power, Hotspur and his uncle Worcester met with Edmund Mortimer and the ferocious Welshman. The final details of their alliance were here to be secured, though the way to comfortable agreement was proving a little thorny with the unruly tongue of Hotspur in full flow. Though he and Glendower complimented each other on the brilliance of their fiery reputations, Hotspur shuffled restlessly when the Welsh lord assured them further that at his birth the frame and huge foundation of the earth had shaken like a coward.

'Why, so it would have done at the same season, if your mother's cat had kittened, though yourself had never been born,' Hotspur remarked, bored. He would most assuredly acknowledge reputations won with visible deeds of valour on the field of war, but echoes of wild Welsh magic simply made him snort in mirthful disbelief.

'I say the earth did shake when I was born,' Glendower glowered at him. 'The front of heaven was full of fiery shapes. These signs have marked me extraordinary . . .'

'I think there's no man speaks better Welsh,' yawned Hotspur, and stood up from the table. Clearly no discussion of any importance would take place here.

'Peace, cousin Percy, you will make him mad,' warned Mortimer. There was too much at stake to let Hotspur have his head and sour the health of their alliance against the king.

'I can call spirits from the vasty deep,' Glendower frowned.

'Why, so can I, or so can any man; but will they come when you call for them?' Hotspur defied him, and each glared angrily, until a sudden chuckle from the Welshman met a grin from Hotspur, and they all sat around the table once again to talk of how they would divide the territory of England between themselves, after the rebellion . . .

Hotspur, however, did not like the portion assigned to him. The wrangling began anew until Hotspur got his way, and finally, all

differences resolved, agreement reached, the meeting ended. Before the night was out the men would leave, Mortimer, Hotspur and Worcester to journey to meet Northumberland and the Scottish Douglas at Shrewsbury. Glendower would follow later . . .

And now the sharp cutting knives of politics were sheathed: their wives joined them, to say farewell and soften the final hour with a sweet Welsh song sung by Glendower's daughter, the new Lady Mortimer, and loving teasing from Hotspur's wife, the Lady Percy, though as she watched her fierce, ungovernable husband go to war, she did not let him see the tear that crept so silently across her cheek . . .

King Henry faced Prince Hal. It seemed to the king that in his hour of need, as rebellion opened its bloody jaws to sever England, when most he needed the loyalty and services of a valiant, honourable son, this heir to the throne instead became more dissolute, clung more persistently to all his low companions and their murky criminal lives, became more like a scourge sent from God to punish the king for his own misdeeds.

He could hardly bear looking at him. Hal stood there for all the world like the young wastrel Richard had, when he, not yet a king, but mere

Henry Bolingbroke had come to seize back his inheritance. And as young Henry Bolingbroke had looked then, so was young Hotspur now, fierce, valiant, quick to the battle when the battle came, heaping bright honours upon himself with every victory . . .

'You,' the king accused his son, 'you are more likely, through fear, to fight against me under Percy's pay, to dog his heels and curtsy at his frowns, to show how much you are degenerate!'

'Do not think so!' Prince Hal burst out, stung finally by the injustice of this accusation to break his silence. 'You shall not find it so! And God forgive them that so much have swayed your majesty's good thoughts away from me! I will redeem all this on Percy's head,' he swore passionately. 'And in the closing of some glorious day be bold to tell you that I am your son! The time will come when I shall make this northern youth exchange his glorious deeds for my indignities!'

There was such a fire in his words, such fury in his vow that he would prove himself against the much-praised Hotspur, that his father's faltering trust was caught, his sorrowing love quickened with sudden hope. Were there, after all, the makings of a king slumbering in this wild young man?

But there was little time to wonder. Already news had come that the rebels were gathering at Shrewsbury. With all speed must the forces of the crown set forth to stop them . . .

At Shrewsbury the rebel lords waited for their forces to be fully gathered. Glendower must still come from Wales, and Hotspur's father, Northumberland, with his powers.

The news, coming suddenly that Northumberland was ill in bed and could not come, was bad. But there was no going back, for the king had already mustered arms and was marching north.

'Where is the king's son, the nimble-footed madcap Prince of Wales and all his comrades?' Hotspur enquired curiously of Sir Richard Vernon who had observed the royal preparations for the war.

'All in arms, all plumed like ostriches, glittering in golden coats, as full of spirit as the month of May,' came Vernon's answer. 'I saw young Harry with his helmet on, gallantly armed, rise from the ground and vault with such ease into his saddle as if an angel dropped down from the heaven . . .'

'Let them come,' cried Hotspur. 'Harry to Harry shall meet and

24

never part till one drop down a corpse!' and even news that Glendower was delayed and would not get to Shrewsbury before the king, could not dampen the prince of honour's thirst for battle. How many in the king's army? Thirty thousand at the very least . . .

'Forty let it be!' Hotspur dared all. To win against such odds would be more glorious, would heap still greater honours on their names . . .

And so the armies gathered in Shrewsbury: as yet, no more than ten thousand rebel men, while towards them marched the massing armies of King Henry's loyal lords.

Falstaff had, on the recommendation of Prince Hal, been given command of a company of footsoldiers, and he was also on his way to Shrewsbury. But the observer, spying the vast knight engaged by the roadside in stowing wine and food in his capacious belly, might have wondered what he'd done with his hundred and fifty soldiers, and why he'd dragged a straggle of miserable beggars all this way to huddle pitifully, more bone than flesh, beside the road while Falstaff ate. The answer was simple: Sir John Falstaff was engaged, as always, in villainy and gluttony at the same time, and he had sold the king's soldiers to line his own fat purse. He had pressed into his army only those rich enough and willing enough to buy themselves out again and in their place, he'd put this ragged band of left-overs.

'How now, blown Jack!' a familiar voice hailed him: the prince riding by en route for his command beside the King. 'Make haste,' Hal yelled. 'Percy is already in the field!'

'Well,' Falstaff shrugged as they rode on and he settled to his meal, 'to the latter end of a fray and the beginning of a feast fits a dull fighter and a keen guest . . .'

The rebel camp blazed with a new argument. Hotspur was all for immediate battle and Douglas agreed with him. Worcester and Vernon were all for waiting till more of their force arrived.

Their argument broke off, for through the night's thin air had come a trumpet's plaintive wail. It heralded the approach of Sir Walter Blunt with an offer from the king. Henry asked to know their grievances and pledged that if he had in any way forgotten their rights, he would put the matter right and pardon all who gathered now against him!

'Well *we* know the king knows at what time to promise,' retorted Hotspur angrily, 'and when to pay,' and to the startled Walter Blunt he poured forth a stream of bitter accusations against the king for broken promises and committed wrongs.

'Shall I return this answer to the king?' demanded Blunt, appalled that even on the brink of bloody war, this impatient young man could not learn the language of negotiation and diplomacy.

The question stopped Hotspur in full flow. He shook his head. 'Not so, Sir Walter: we'll withdraw awhile. Go to the king, and in the morning early shall my uncle bring him our answer . . .'

'I wish you would accept of grace and love,' said Blunt.

'And may be so we shall,' replied Hotspur, eager for this messenger of the despised king to leave, that they might all the quicker come to their decision.

Beneath a bloody rising sun a pale day shivered in a blustering wind. King Henry, armoured for the fray, awaited the rebels' answer with Prince Hal by his side.

It was brought by Worcester, who masked nothing of his discontent, and spilled the catalogue of accusations more bitterly than even Hotspur's words to Blunt. Grimly the king heard it. There was little hope of peace before these hates . . .

Prince Hal stepped forward. 'Tell your nephew,' he said to Worcester quietly, 'the Prince of Wales joins in with all the world in praise of Henry Percy. I do not think a braver gentleman, more daring or more bold, is now alive. For my part, I may speak it to my shame, I have been a truant to chivalry. Yet I am content that he shall take the odds of his great name, and I will, to save the blood on either side, try fortune with him in a single fight.'

Proudly the king heard his son's brave challenge, but laid a restraining hand upon his arm. There was too much at stake to leave its outcome to the skill and courage of a single man. And he knew how much greater was the army gathering to defend the crown, than that which steeled itself to challenge it.

He repeated his offer to the rebels: a pardon if they all lay down their arms, if not, a bloody war to end their threat to him.

'It will not be accepted,' Hal shook his head, 'Douglas and Hotspur both together are confident against the world in arms!'

The king's voice rose across the assembled lords, 'Every leader to his command, for on their answer we will set on them.'

'Hal,' said Falstaff gloomily, moving towards his friend. 'I wish it were bed-time, Hal, and all well.'

'Why, you owe God a death,' declared the prince with a grin.

'It is not due yet,' complained Falstaff indignantly. 'I would be loathe to pay him before his day! Well, no matter,' he assured himself, 'honour pricks me on.' But with this thought there came another. 'But how if honour prick me *off* when I come on?' He paused, struck dumb by this grotesque prospect. 'Can honour set a leg?' he wondered. 'No. Or an arm? No. Or take away the grief of a wound? No. Honour has no skill in surgery, then? No. What is honour? A word. What is in that word honour? Air. Who had it? He that died on Wednesday.' He shook his head in disbelief: the more one sang this word 'honour', so much loved by all the world, the hollower was its tune. He shrugged, 'I'll have none of it!' but off he lumbered to lead his ragged warriors to the fray.

Worcester never told Hotspur of King Henry's offer of a pardon for the rebels. He knew too well that there would never be a reconciliation between himself and the king, and that the pardon would not be for him. With a single word, Worcester might have spared the lives of thousands. He chose instead to plunge them all into the jaws of war.

And as they poised on the brink of battle, even headstrong Hotspur felt the shiver of their fate pass like a grave's chill across the field. He thought of the Prince of Wales' challenge, and wished suddenly that the quarrel *could* lay only on their heads, and that no one but he and Hal should pant in vicious battle on this day . . .

But even as the thunder of the king's attack swelled in the air, he pushed the thoughts away. He raised his sword aloft. 'If we live, we live to tread on kings; if die, brave death, when princes die with us!'

And now the pale trembling morning was swallowed in the stench of battle dust, the clash of murderous steel and sickening slice of sword blades into flesh and bone. From all sides came the shrieks of men who struggled to and fro across the land grown slippery with blood . . .

Lord Douglas searched with grim determination for the king, for he had sworn that England's monarch would this day fall to him. He found a thousand monarchs, sprouting like Hydra's heads, for the king had dressed many in his armour to confuse the enemy.

'Now, my sword,' yelled Douglas, felling one and swinging round to find another. 'I'll murder all his wardrobe, piece by piece, until I meet the king!'

Falstaff, sidling across the battlefield, had lost all but three of his hundred and fifty ragamuffin warriors. He stumbled across the bloody corpse and peered at it. 'I like not such grinning honour,' he said. 'Give me life . . .'

Meanwhile Douglas had found the real king and being the younger man and much strengthened in recent battle, he was gaining ground upon the panting monarch . . .

With a yell of challenge, the Prince of Wales appeared and fought off Douglas who fled before the furious onslaught. Prince Hal held out his hand and helped his father up. With almost forgotten pride and gratitude Henry looked into his brave son's face and thought of all the years of hurt and anger wiped away this day. But still the battle raged about them, and with swift words of new commands, the king left Hal.

It was then that Hotspur found him. The Harry of the north faced the Harry of the south, and each knew that the moment of grim reckoning was here.

'Think not, Percy, to share with me in glory any more,' said Prince Hal, quietly. 'Two stars keep not their motion in one sphere, nor can one England brook a double reign of Harry Percy and the Prince of Wales.'

'Nor shall it, Harry,' Hotspur cried, 'for the hour has come to end the one of us!'

And so they fought, and it was as though all hopes and fears, all honour, valour, loyalties and hates that fired that field of war that day gathered on the swords of these two panting men . . .

Unnoticed, Falstaff had been sliding by, and transfixed by the sight of Hal in deathly struggle with his bitter rival, hovered, to see the outcome and to egg his young prince on. So it was that he saw the arrival of Douglas too late to heave his clanking armoured bulk into a run. Instead he threw several hefty blows in the direction of the ferocious Scot, and then with a shriek of dreadful pain, fell in a thunderous clatter to the ground and lay still. Douglas rushed into the billowing dust to look for kings again.

28

And Hal pierced Hotspur to the heart. The brave Harry of the north crumpled to the ground and lay before the Harry of the south. He knew that it would not be long before this Harry would be Harry of all.

'You have robbed me of my youth!' he gasped. 'I am dust, and food for . . .'

'For worms, brave Percy,' Prince Hal spoke the words for him, for Hotspur had gasped his final breath. For a while Hal stood looking down at him, and then he knelt to cover the mangled face of death with royal plumes from his own helmet. How small was life, shrunk in an instant into death! 'When this body did contain a spirit, a kingdom for it was too small a space,' he murmured. 'But now two paces of the vilest earth is room enough!'

He rose, and as he turned, spied Falstaff.

'What, old acquaintance,' he burst out, 'could not all this flesh keep in a little life? Poor Jack, farewell. I could have better spared a better man . . .'

The prince had gone. Silence reigned about the fallen Hotspur and the corpse of Falstaff. Then in the fat man's corpse an eye opened. It rolled up and down, spying cautiously. It swivelled from side to side. No one about. He could safely come alive again.

He sat up. 'To fake dying, when a man thereby lives, is to be no fake, but the true and perfect image of life indeed,' he announced sagely. 'The better part of valour is discretion, in which better part I have saved my life!' But being so much impressed with the skills of faking death, it occurred to him that Hotspur too might be a skilful man. 'I'll make sure of him, yes, and swear I killed him.' He drew his sword. 'Nobody sees me,' and he stabbed dead Hotspur in the thigh.

With that he hoisted the fallen hero on his back. Unfortunately, his panting efforts were disturbed by the return of Hal with other lords, all come to fetch the bodies. Open-mouthed, Hal gaped, unable to believe he really saw Poor Jack risen so miraculously from the dead.

Falstaff shrugged nonchalantly. He threw Hotspur's body casually on the ground. 'There is Percy,' he announced. 'If your father will do me any honour, so let it be. If not, let him kill the next Percy himself. I look to be either earl or duke, I can assure you.'

'Why, Percy I killed myself and saw you dead!' exclaimed the prince.

'Did you,' wondered Falstaff in amazement. 'Lord, Lord, how this world is given to lying! I grant you I was down and out of breath, and so was he, but we rose both at an instant and fought a long hour by Shrewsbury clock.'

'This is the strangest tale that ever I heard,' said one lord.

'This is the strangest fellow,' Prince Hal told him, laughing, and he turned to Falstaff, 'Come, bring your luggage nobly on your back. And for my part, if a lie may do you grace, I'll gild it with the happiest terms I have!'

Across the battlefield a trumpet peeled. 'The rebels' trumpet sounds retreat; the day is ours,' cried Hal. 'Come, let us to the field to see what friends are living, who are dead,' and off went the bruised and bloodied warriors of the king, to measure loss and gain . . .

'I'll follow, as they say, for reward,' said Falstaff to no one in particular. He threw his shoulders back, sucked in his sagging belly as best he could, and tried to look as might the greatest hero of the hour, he who had killed the invincible Hotspur and saved the day. And contorted by this mammoth effort, he sailed away on the crest of his new-stolen glory.

Seven thousand men lay dead across the reeking fields of Shrewsbury. And yet, although the day was won, young Percy dead and Douglas captured, their work was still not done. Mortimer, Glendower, and the Duke of Northumberland were still in arms . . . there were more battles to be won. To this end, the king split his powers: one army towards York, to meet Northumberland and the Archbishop of York, while he and his son Hal, the valiant Prince of Wales, would bend their march towards the mountain strongholds of Glendower in Wales . . .

Henry the Fifth

King Henry IV was dead. Although the endless civil strife of his uneasy reign had never claimed his life, year by year the troubled king grew weaker, drained by a disease which at last bore him away. Hal, that prince of boisterous wildness, of riots, banqueting and sports, had received the call of state and in the year 1413, he mounted to the throne of England as King Henry V.

The country watched and doubted, but questioning was short, and wonderment was great: no sooner had the breath of life fled from his father's body than a new spirit seemed to fill the prince. Like a gloriously rising sun, he had emerged from behind the clouds and mists that veiled him. Even as the crown of England settled on his head, there seemed to flow from him a new strength, a sharp clarity of purpose, a brain and heart devoted without pause to the stern offices of ruling England, a mind equipped, though no one could see how, to untie the dangerous knots of politics as though he had done it all his life.

This king had studied people in the muddy by-ways of his youth, those gadding days when old Falstaff and young Poins had been the subject of his thoughts and object of his energies, and though these raucous souls were far from the halls of government in which he walked, all banished from his side, those years, those people, had given a roundness to his vision that stretched beyond the walls of palaces and council chambers . . .

Now other questions demanded answers from the royal mind, and there were several: the bishops were restless beneath the threat of a new law that would dispossess the Church of half its enormous wealth and place it in the treasury of the crown. And the question of the throne of France loomed large, for English kings were tied by birth and blood to the monarchy of France, and for nearly a hundred years the claim of

England's kings to France's realm had driven many to make war on that country so narrowly split from England's soil by the grey waters of the Channel.

The bishops, being men of power who struggled for the survival of their Church as though it were a kingdom, made offers to the king: if he would put aside the law proposed, they would put forward a greater sum than Church had ever given to any other king, to be used to wage another war to claim the crown of France for England's king.

And now King Henry V prepared to hear the arguments on all these questions: the bishops waited for their audience, and so too did an ambassador from the heir to the crown of France, the young Dauphin.

First it was the bishops' turn: before King Henry faced the voice of France, he wished to know, with absolute certainty, how stood the law upon the question of his rights to any claim upon the territory or throne of France. They stood before him, the Archbishop of Canterbury and the Bishop of Ely, eager, as he saw, to press their argument for war on France and so divert the question of the seizure of the Church's wealth.

He looked at them long and hard, and in that look there was a world of threat. They must not mould or mask their argument with lies, with half-truths that hid doubtful claims. 'Take heed,' he warned them. 'Take heed how you awake our sleeping sword of war: we charge you, in the name of God, take heed; for never two such kingdoms did contend without much fall of blood.'

The argument put forward by the Archbishop of Canterbury was long and serious, and it had much to do with the long history of the birth and death of kingdoms across the Channel and the French law on who should and should not inherit France's crown. It was they argued, false . . .

'May I with right and conscience make this claim?' Henry demanded a clear and unclouded answer from the archbishop.

He could, they swore: his claim to the throne of France came from his grandfather, King Edward III of England, son of Isabella of France, daughter of the French King Philip IV. He owed it, in all honour, to the name of Edward and his great-uncle the Black Prince who had fought bloodily on France's soil to press the claim to that crown.

'You are their heir: you sit upon their throne,' the Bishop of Ely leant his voice to the persuasion. 'The blood and courage that renowned them runs in your veins. And my liege is in the very May-morn of his youth, ripe for exploits and mighty enterprises.'

The Duke of Exeter, uncle to the king, spoke now. 'Your brother kings and monarchs of the earth do all expect that you should rouse yourself as did the former lions of your blood.'

And then the Earl of Westmoreland, 'They know your grace has cause and means and might!'

King Henry looked at all of them, each one fired with an eagerness to press the cause of war against France, and certain of the justice of his claim, though he could see as well that justice was not the only fuel to their argument: too often wars abroad were used as remedy for unrest here at home, focusing discontent and energies upon a distant foe . . . and even as he thought of this, he thought too of his dead father, that king whose reign had been so wracked with rivalries and civil discontent. 'Be it your course to busy giddy minds with foreign quarrels . . .' he had urged his son, as he lay dying. Now Henry V reflected that here at home there was much need of a defence against the Scots, who had formed a habit, when England went to war with France, of pouring across the northern borders of the realm . . .

The lords, however, were confident: defence at home could be maintained against any threat. 'Therefore to France, my liege,' urged the Archbishop of Canterbury. 'Divide your happy England into four; take one quarter into France. If we, with three times that power left at home cannot defend our own doors, let our nation lose the name of hardiness and policy.'

And still the King looked at them, weighing each word for truth and falsity, for gain and loss . . .

Suddenly he made up his mind. Of the justice of his claim to France against its present monarchy, he had no doubt. And there would be, he judged, much strengthening of England and its king to be gained from victories in war. The years of restless instability that clouded all the years of his father's reign were not to be repeated under him. King Henry V, at war abroad, and returning from that war victorious, was going to give such glory, honour, prestige to England's king that loyalty to him must follow, and from that, peace on England's soil!

He would to war in France, to take it, or beneath the might of England's army, break it all to pieces; to win, or die. And now, his decision taken, he was well prepared to hear the messages brought from the Dauphin in answer to a claim he'd made to certain dukedoms in France.

The Dauphin's answer was a simple one, and brooked no misunderstanding. The Dauphin said, and the ambassador repeated the words carefully, 'you savour too much of your youth, and bids you know that there's nothing in France that can be won with a nimble dance. He therefore sends you, more fitting for your spirit, this treasure, and desires you let the dukedoms that you claim hear no more of you.'

King Henry gave no answer. Even before the speech was over he could hear the trumpet's call to war ringing in his inward ear. He waited calmly while the ambassador unpacked the package placed before them on the ground.

'What treasure?' he enquired.

'Tennis-balls,' replied the ambassador rolling them on to the floor.

King Henry smiled. 'We are glad the Dauphin is so pleasant with us,' he said easily, as though he had received the most generous birthday present in the world. 'His present and your pains we thank you for:

when we have matched our rackets to these balls, we will in France, by God's grace, play a set shall strike his father's crown into the hazard!' He waited for the laughter in the Court to die, and then began again. But now his smile had faded and in its place the king's young face grew hard beyond its years and in his eyes there came that glitter of determination so like his father's as he'd swept all before him on his march towards England's throne.

'And tell the pleasant prince,' he said quietly, 'this mock of his has turned his tennis balls to gunstones, and some are yet unborn that shall have cause to curse the Dauphin's scorn! And tell the Dauphin I am coming on, to revenge me as I may and to put forth my rightful hand in a well-hallowed cause. His jest will savour but of shallow wit when thousands weep!'

Thus did England set its sights on war, and all the country's youth threw off its gaudy clothes of pleasure for the glint of armour, all images of blood and death and misery on smoking battlefields swallowed by the fire of honour's call to war for possession of the lands and crown of France.

The French learned of the preparations and looked for ways to turn England's king aside: three corrupt men they found, one Richard, Earl of Cambridge, the second, close friend of the king, Lord Scroop of Masham and the third, Sir Thomas Grey of Northumberland. For payment of French gold these three conspired to kill Henry before he could set sail for France.

The king learned of their plot, and in Southampton as his army embarked, prepared to trap the traitors. With easy courtesy he and his lords sat in the council chamber and talked with them of the war to come, and of the loyalties of all who joined with the enterprise.

Unsuspecting, they followed on the path he laid, and with fair words they flattered him. 'Never was a monarch better feared and loved than is your majesty,' said Cambridge, with a fawning smile, 'There's not, I think, a subject that sits in heart-grief and uneasiness under the sweet shade of your government.'

'True,' added Grey, 'those that were your father's enemies do serve you with hearts of duty and of zeal.'

'So service shall with steeled sinews toil to do your grace incessant services,' added Scroop.

The king nodded, with a studied calm about his face and a smile that seemed to say he knew them all; and so he did, though not the way they understood . . .

He turned and gestured to his uncle Exeter; swift orders given to free a man imprisoned yesterday who had shouted at the king and complained of him. 'We consider,' said the king, 'it was excess of wine that set him on, and on more thought, we pardon him.'

'That's mercy, but too much confidence,' protested Scroop, the traitor who did not know he was unmasked. 'Let him be punished, lest his example breed more of such a kind!'

'Alas,' exclaimed Henry, 'your too much love and care of me are heavy pleas against this poor wretch! If little faults, proceeding from such drunkenness shall not be winked at, how shall we stretch our eye when capital crimes, chewed, swallowed, and digested appear before us?'

The plotters, opening their mouths confidently to continue with their arguments for punishment, paled at the question. It cut too near the bone, and even they in their smooth self-confidence could feel it. But the king, it seemed, was merely making general comments, and had already moved on, signalling for some papers: their orders, they assumed, for their commands in France.

'Read them,' said the king, 'and know *I* know your worthiness.' He turned away, 'My lord of Westmoreland, and uncle Exeter, we will aboard tonight.'

They took the papers with a bow, and opened them. Into their faces, smiling, smooth and confident, there crept a greyness . . .

Henry had turned, and watched them now. 'Why, how now, gentlemen!' he said grimly. 'What do you see in those papers that you lose so much complexion? Look you, how they change!' he marvelled to his assembled lords.

Bloodless lips whispered, but made no sound. They could not shift their eyes from the evidence, on paper, of their treachery against their king, the evidence that they had sold his life to France.

Cambridge found words first. 'I do confess my fault and so submit me to your highness' mercy,' he whispered in a voice as pale as his face.

'To which we all appeal,' whispered Grey and Scroop.

King Henry laughed, but there was no mirth in the sound. 'The mercy that was quick in us until now, *by your own counsel* is suppressed and killed! See you, my princes and my noble peers, these English monsters!' He got up from his seat, and came to stand behind the three of them. In silence, trembling visibly, they sat with downcast eyes. Slowly, behind Cambridge and then Grey, he moved, and then behind Lord Scroop he stopped. This man, more than the others, had been close to him. 'What shall I say to you, Lord Scroop? You cruel, ungrateful, savage and inhuman creature!' He shook his head, and for a moment turned away to hide the working passion in his face, for in this friend he had seen that blend of duty, learning and nobility that drew from Henry infinite trust.

'I will weep for you,' he said, and fell to silence. All waited for the movement of the king.

And suddenly he swung away. 'Arrest them! Hear your sentence. You have sold your king to slaughter, his princes and his peers to servitude, his subjects to oppression and contempt and his whole kingdom into desolation. We our kingdom's safety must so care for, whose ruin you have sought, that to her laws we deliver you! Get you therefore, miserable wretches, to your death!'

In silence guards came in, and in silence led the three away. Henry took his seat again. Still no one spoke and the king stared deep into some inward thought. But when, a moment later he slapped the table with his hand, all darkness had left his gaze. 'Now lords, for France!' he said.

But even as King Henry shook away the blackness of his anger at friendship so savagely betrayed, there was another friendship lost which had brought about another death. The old companion of his youth, the great jovial rogue of villainy and gluttony, of comradeship and a world of shared merriment, the old fat knight, Sir John Falstaff, was dead. He had died, so people said, from heartache at his banishment from Hal, that merry prince, who had walked through a door through which the monstrous shape of Falstaff could not squeeze, the door of royalty and stately duty, the door that opened on the throne of England.

It was even on the day of Prince Hal's coronation as the king that Falstaff had been caught behind that slamming door, and he had shivered; a cold day it had been, icy cold, even deathly cold to Falstaff. Though neither insults, nor lies, nor even the bloody swords of fiercest warriors could hurt his massive hide, he had been pierced to the quick by the great echo of that sharply slamming door, though Hal had said that he *would* close it, and Falstaff had heard him say it. Good king might Henry be, but to old Falstaff he had nevertheless betrayed a friendship. And old Jack, though he had worn it all with good enough grace at first, had in the end become Poor Jack, and died.

In France, at King Charles VI's Court, the news of Henry's preparations for the war fired swift defences of the towns and regions of the land. The Dauphin, though, was scornful of the threat from England, 'she is so idly kinged, her sceptre so fantastically borne by a vain, giddy, shallow, humorous youth . . .'

Others, however, had better knowledge of this king who hit back tennis-balls with easy grace and humour and in the same breath threw down the gauntlet of war, this king bred of Edward the Black Prince's blood, whose victories on France's soil had slain many a Frenchman. And swiftly on the heels of their debate, came messengers from England's king: the Earl of Exeter carrying Henry's claim to the throne of France and his request, to avert the war, that France's king resign the crown and kingdom now.

'Or else what follows?' asked the King of France.

'Bloody constraint!' said Exeter, 'for if you hide the crown even in your hearts, there will he rake for it. In fierce tempest is he coming, in thunder and in earthquake, and bids you deliver up the crown, and to take mercy on the poor souls for whom this hungry war opens his vasty jaws, and on your head turning the widows' tears, the orphans' cries, the dead mens' blood, the pining maidens' groans for husbands, fathers and betrothed lovers that shall be swallowed in this war . . .

At Southampton pier the English king embarked: eight thousand men, and fifteen hundred ships flying silken streamers in the wind and surging through the waves towards France and war, for the possession of a crown, a throne, a land, to raise high the name of England in the book of victory . . .

At France's port of Harfleur, standing across the Channel from England's shores, the English king and army landed, and there laid siege, their cannons trained on Harfleur's walls, his army mustered round, imprisoning the city's citizens within. There Henry received the King of France's answer to his absolute demands: in lieu of crown, the

French king offered his daughter Katherine in marriage and a clutch of minor dukedoms.

The offer did not please the English king. His breaching towers rolled in to scale the city's walls, the gunner's match was touched to cannons, and the war began.

'Once more unto the breach, dear friends, once more,' with rallying cry King Henry led on, 'or close the wall up with our English dead. When the blast of war blows in our ears, then imitate the action of the tiger, stiffen the sinews, summon up the blood, hold hard the breath and bend up every spirit to his full height. On, on, you noblest English! Follow your spirit, and upon this charge cry 'God for Harry, England and St George!'

'On, on, on, on, on! to the breach, to the breach!' came the echoing cry from the crimson sweating face of one well-known to England's king, had he but seen him. Before Harfleur's smoking walls, among the soldiers scrabbling to the breach beneath the ringing cry of king and lords all charging for a crown, there was one Lieutenant Bardolph, known well to Henry in his greener days with jolly Falstaff in the taverns of Eastcheap. There was also one Corporal Nym, one Ensign Pistol, and one boy, all of whom were panting in the general direction of the fray, but faltered, staggered, and sank, breathing heavily, to the ground.

'The knocks are too hot,' wheezed Corporal Nym, who was reluctant to part with the only life he had, there being, as he explained, no replacement for it.

'Knocks go and come; God's vassals drop and die;
And sword and shield,
In bloody field,
Do win immortal fame,' sang Pistol irreverently.

'Would I were in an alehouse in London!' sighed the boy. 'I would give all my fame for a pot of ale and safety.'

'And I,' carolled Pistol,
'If wishes would prevail with me,
My purpose should not fail with me,
But thither would I fly.'

But this brief interlude was swiftly broken by the arrival of a short, fierce Welshman, Captain Fluellen by name, who had no time for soldiers resting on the ground while England's king scaled the city walls for glory.

'Up to the breach, you dogs,' he yelled, 'On, on, you scoundrels,' driving them forward.

'Be merciful, great duke to men of mould,' squealed Pistol, 'Abate your rage, abate your manly rage, abate your rage great duke!' and with Nym and Bardolph hard on his heels, all fled, all that is, except the boy, who had observed Bardolph, adept at never fighting, Pistol, who could whip his tongue about as sharp as any weapon, but kept his sword firmly sheathed, and Nym, who was drunk more often than sober: these three had carried the villainies of Eastcheap to the wars, and were occupied far more energetically in keeping their hand in with the stealing and the pick-pocketing, than with the bloody war to gain the crown of France, though it appeared to the boy that all was more for love than money, their pilfering being in the nature of lute-cases and coal-shovels, of which the boy was hard put to see the sense, and so determined to escape their clutches before he was many hours older . . .

The citizens of Harfleur, weakening by the day beneath the merciless battering of the English army, called for a parley: high on the walls the governor and citizens looked down on Henry and the serried ranks of English soldiers spread below.

'If I begin the battery once again, I will not leave Harfleur till in her ashes she lies buried!' Henry warned, 'Therefore you men of Harfleur, take pity on your town and on your people while yet my soldiers are in my command,' and with the glowering eye of one who knew his absolute power and knew that he had conquered, he painted such a picture of savagery, of waste and desolation, of murder, riot, looting and pitiless villainy as made all who heard it quake and never doubt that to defy his powers would bring this hellish fate swooping like a god of vengeance to their town.

'What say you?' he demanded. 'Will you yield, and this avoid, or guilty in defence, be thus destroyed?'

'Great king, we yield our town and lives,' the answer came. 'Enter our gates. Dispose of us and ours . . .'

'Come, uncle Exeter,' King Henry said. 'Go you and enter Harfleur; there remain and fortify it strongly against the French: use mercy on them all.'

His uncle in command of the defeated town, Henry turned his powers north. Winter was coming on, and though this victory here was absolute, sickness was growing among his soldiers. His aim must be to reach Calais, for that city had been conquered many years before and was in English hands. There might they rest and gather strength for further conquest.

In the palace of the King of France, report of Henry's victory at Harfleur broke any belief that England's king was merely playing at war. And swiftly on the heels of this they heard that, marching northward towards Calais, he had already passed the River Somme.

'Dieu de batailles!' exclaimed the Lord Constable of France, 'where have they this mettle? Is not their climate foggy, raw and dull, on whom the sun looks pale, killing their fruit with frowns? Oh, for honour of our land let us not hang like roping icicles upon our houses' thatch, while a more frosty people sweats drops of gallant youth in our rich fields!'

'By faith and honour,' complained the Dauphin, 'our madams mock at us and plainly say our mettle is bred out and they will give themselves to English youth!'

'They bid us go to the English dancing schools,' protested the Duke of Bourbon. 'They say our grace is only in our heels and that we are most lofty runaways!'

But news had also come that sickness overwhelmed the English army, and they were growing weaker. They must be cut off from their path to Calais, for once in Calais walls they could recover, muster their strength, and emerge again for further conquest. 'Up princes!' urged the king, 'and with spirit of honour edged sharper than your swords, hurry to the field. High dukes, great princes, barons, lords and knights, bar Harry England that sweeps through our land with pennons painted in the blood of Harfleur! Go down upon him, you have power enough, and in a captive chariot into Rouen bring him our prisoner. Now forth, lord constable and princes all, and quickly bring us word of England's fall . . .'

The English force had reached Agincourt and beneath the gaze of the high castle walls they were encamped. Ensign Pistol was most anxious, searching out that fierce Welshman, Captain Fluellen with an earnest plea: Bardolph (a soldier, firm and sound of heart, and of buxom valour, he assured the captain) had been caught looting a church and would be shortly for the looter's fate: to be hanged by his neck until dead.

'Fortune is Bardolph's foe and frowns on him,' wailed Pistol, summoning all his eloquence. 'Therefore go speak: the Duke of Exeter will hear your voice; let not Bardolph's vital thread be cut with edge of penny cord and vile reproach. Speak, captain for his life!'

His wails and fulsome pleas fell all on deaf ears. A looter was no more than a looter to Captain Fluellen, whose sense of bravery and military decorum was modelled on the glory of the Roman army, great Pompey, Julius Caesar, Mark Antony and all: discipline against the undisciplined riot of looting must be used!

'Die and be damned!' yelled Pistol, incensed at this faithless abandonment of friendship and rushed away to try some other course.

'It is well,' shrugged Fluellen, and turned to the more interesting matter of the arrival of the king who came to view the camp. Though he did confide, amongst several other reports, that one Lieutenant

Bardolph was shortly to be hanged, and he gave such a description of the man that there could be no doubt that such a Bardolph was the unmistakable Bardolph of Eastcheap and fat John Falstaff, and of King Henry's former days as wild Prince Hal.

There was no hint of any memories on Henry's face. He surveyed the camp, the absolute military commander for whom only the iron will of discipline, obedience and firm control had any voice, and with slow deliberation he nodded, 'We would have all such offenders so cut off: and we give express charge that in our marches through the country there be nothing seized from the villages, nothing taken but what is paid for, none of the French abused . . .'

There came a sudden interruption: to King Henry of England from the King of France, a message. 'Thus says my king,' the ambassador began. 'Say to Harry of England this: though we seemed dead, we did but sleep: advantage is a better soldier than rashness. England shall repent this folly, see his weakness, and admire our sufferance. Bid him therefore consider of his ransom, which must equal the losses we have borne, the subjects we have lost, the disgrace we have digested. For our losses, his treasury is too poor, for the spilling of our blood, the muster of his kingdom too faint a number, and for our disgrace, his own person, kneeling at our feet, but a weak and worthless satisfaction . . .'

'Turn back,' was England's answer, 'and tell the king I do not seek him now but could be willing to march on to Calais without hindrance. My people are with sickness much enfeebled, my numbers lessened . . . Tell him,' said Henry quietly, 'we *will* come on, though France himself stand in our way. If we may pass, we will; if we be hindered, we shall discolour your tawny ground with your red blood. The sum of all our answer is but this: we would not seek a battle as we are, nor, as we are, will we shun it . . .'

The night was drawing in. Not fifteen hundred paces from the English camp, the massive French force gathered, confident and fresh and well provided, the lords and princes bragging about the merits of their horses and exchanging jokes about the battle that would come with the mad-brained English king who persisted with his foolish march through France, though weakened by illness, long marches and the colder days.

'When I bestride my horse, I soar, I am a hawk: he trots the air; the earth sings when he touches it; the basest horn of his hoof is more musical than the pipe of Hermes!' said the Dauphin. 'Will it never be day?' he complained. 'I will trot tomorrow a mile, and my way shall be paved with English faces! It is midnight,' he announced suddenly. 'I'll go arm myself!'

'He longs to eat the English,' was the dry comment of Lord Rambures, watching their exotic royal heir rush away.

'Would it were day!' sighed the lord constable, 'Alas, poor Harry of England! He longs not for the dawning as we do.'

'Foolish curs that run winking into the mouth of a Russian bear and have their heads crushed like rotten apples!' exclaimed the Duke of Orleans scornfully. 'You may as well say that's a valiant flea that dares eat his breakfast on the lip of a lion!'

'Come,' interrupted the lord constable, 'now is the time to arm: come, shall we about it?'

'It is now two o'clock,' nodded Orleans. 'But let me see, by ten we shall have each a hundred Englishmen . . .'

Across the darkened landscape the camp-fires of the two armies flickered; flame answered flame, the hum and clatter of the soldiers' movement in the camps echoed each the other. Horses neighed across the night air, and it was a shrill, chill sound. The French, confident of their great numbers against the shrunken English force, played dice and drew bets on the deaths of Englishmen.

In the English camp, the bloom of glory's call which had drawn them cheering across the sea to Harfleur's walls had faded. Their faces, white as bone in the dank hours of night, stared hollow-cheeked towards their looming fate.

Then through their ranks a figure moved: the royal captain of this ruined band, the king. Quietly he walked from fire to fire, from sentinel to sentinel, from tent to tent, calling them brothers, friends and countrymen, giving no sign of fear that a dread army barred their path to safety. Nor did he show the greyness of exhaustion as all others did, but with a look as fresh and clear as a spring morning, with cheerful smiles and courtesy, he urged them to take heart, and as he passed, the soldiers, pining and pale before, plucked some comfort from his looks, the icing grip of fear began to thaw . . .

The dawn came closer. Alone in his pavilion, unwatched now by the lords and soldiers who drew such heart from him, Henry brooded on

45

the dangers looming. He and the lords of England had chosen war, and few soldiers there had not flown on wings across the Channel to fight, as all would say, for England's power. But now they all reaped the harvest of that choice, and there was no going back. He, the king, had brought them here, and on his strength must their lives rest. And though the outward king was strong and certain in his cause, the inward king stirred restlessly, uneasy beneath the grimness of his responsibility for his own choice.

And in these final hours before the dawn, he wrapped a borrowed cloak about his shoulders, and so disguised, he went again among his men, not as the king, but as a soldier, unnamed and unknown, to hear his soldiers' hearts, and find some new calm in his own.

'Qui va la?' Pistol accosted him, busy practising his tongue in French.

'A friend,' said Henry. 'A gentleman of the company. What are you?'

'As good a gentleman as the emperor,' Pistol assured him.

'Then you are better than the king,' said the disguised king.

'The king's a fine fellow, and a heart of gold, a lad of life, an imp of fame; of fist most valiant,' declared Pistol eloquently. 'I kiss his dirty shoe, and from the heart-string I love the bully. Do you know Fluellen?' he demanded, for no particular reason except that that military gentleman figured large in his catalogue of villains since Bardolph's hanging alongside Corporal Nym for the crime of looting. 'Tell him I'll knock his leek about his head upon Saint David's day!' Pistol declared, bristling for some dire insult with which to flatten the Welshman, and away he went, his conscience unclouded by any twisting choices for good or evil as might trouble the disguised monarch threading his way through that waiting camp.

The king, alone again, drew his cloak still tighter round his shoulders and moved on. By the dim light of a small fire, three soldiers sat and watched the sky paling in the east.

'Who goes there?' demanded one, by name of Williams.

'A friend,' said Henry, 'serving in the company of Sir Thomas Erpingham,' and he sat beside them, warming his hands by the dying fire.

'What thinks he of our situation?' Williams asked.

'That we be men wrecked upon a sand that look to be washed off at the next tide,' said Henry, the confidence of the bright king abandoned in the light of the dimly flickering fire.

'He has not told his thoughts to the king?' enquired another, Bates, with curiosity.

'No, nor should he,' said the disguised king, 'for I think the king is but a man, as I am, the violet smells to him as it does to me. His ceremonies put aside, in his nakedness he appears as but a man. Therefore, when he sees reason for fear, as we do, his fears are the same as ours; no man should give him fear, lest he, by showing it, should dishearten his army.'

'He may show what outward courage he will,' muttered Bates with passion, 'but I believe he could wish himself in the Thames up to the neck, and so I wish he were, and I by him, so long as we were out of here!'

There was silence, and Henry stared into the flames of the fire between them. He had listened not merely to the words but to the passion too. Such passion, on the morrow, would be the passion of defeat. 'I think he would not wish himself anywhere but where he is,' spoke Henry, bringing a firm certainty into his voice.

'Then I wish he were alone; so should he be sure to be ransomed and many poor men's lives saved,' said Bates bitterly.

The king looked at all of them, his eyes searching the soldiers' faces one by one. This then, was truth as well, as true as the call of honour, nobility and valour raised by lords and princes and archbishops. He spoke again, 'I could not die anywhere so contented as in the king's company, his cause being just and his quarrel honourable.'

'That's more than we know,' Williams shook his head, and though he spoke without heat, there was anger in his tone. 'And if the cause be not good, the king has a heavy reckoning to make, when all those legs and arms and heads, chopped off in a battle shall join together on Doomsday and cry together, "We died at such a place!" some swearing, some crying for a surgeon, some upon their wives left poor behind them, some upon the debts they owe, some upon their children rawly left. I am afraid few die well that die in a battle, and if these men do not die well, it will be a black matter for the king that led them to it!'

'The king is not bound to answer for the particular endings of his soldiers,' Henry said. 'Every subject's duty is the king's, but every subject's soul is his own.' Yet even as he said it, and believed it, he also knew that it was no answer to the men whose blood seeped out and drained into the bitter soil of battlefields.

Around the fire, merely embers now, as the pale day rose in the eastern sky, they sat in silence, thinking of the questions of a man's responsibility for what he did and what he'd done.

'Tis certain,' murmured Williams, 'every man that dies ill, this ill is upon his own head, the king is not to answer for it.'

Bates sighed heavily, but in that sigh of resignation, the mood of black defeat exhaled, as it had done on many another battlefield, before and after. 'I do not desire he should answer for me, and yet I determine to fight lustily for him!' he declared rising from the fire.

'I myself heard the king say he would not give in,' King Henry assured them, rising too, to meet the battle-day.

Williams snorted. 'Aye, he said so, to make us fight cheerfully: but when *our* throats are cut, he may be ransomed, and we never the wiser!'

'If I live to see it, I will never trust his word after!' Henry protested, stung by such blatant dismissal of his own honour.

'You'll never trust his word after!' scorned Williams. 'Come, it is a foolish saying!'

48

'Be friends, you English fools, be friends,' urged Bates, 'we have French quarrels enough!' and on that note the English soldiers went to fight the battle which they did not want to fight, but fight they would, and bravely too, but not for honour now, nor crowns or thrones, but for survival.

And Henry churned the argument of that paling dawn around his mind. There was no answer and no escape from it: as a man he might take on responsibility for his own deeds: as king he carried too the responsibilities of all those choices made by other men from loyalty, love, duty and obedience to the grand, golden glory of a king; and what was a king, when all was said and done, but a thing of ceremony, a man that held a sword, a mace, a crown, and wore a robe of gold and pearl, to sit upon a throne in pomp and circumstance; and what was this ceremony but a thing of no greater substance than its outward show to create fear and awe in other men? And yet this man of ceremony, this king, must then take on the heavy weight of all men's choices flowing so from those he made himself. And where could such a man, as king, find rest and ease?

And wrestling now with all the heavy burden of his choices, King Henry knelt, to pray, investing in that prayer all hopes and fears of that grim night of reckoning. 'Oh God of battles,' he prayed, 'steel my soldiers' hearts; possess them not with fear . . .'

'To horse, to horse, you gallant princes,' came the Lord Constable of France's rallying cry across the camp. 'Do but behold the poor and starved band, and your fair show shall suck away their souls, leaving them but shells and husks of men! There is scarce blood enough in all their sickly veins to give each axe a stain!'

Jeering, they viewed the dwindled English force, with ragged banners fluttering and horses thin with hunger . . .

'Shall we go send them dinners and fresh suits, and after fight with them,' the Dauphin yelled to laughter.

In the English camp the commanders gathered, and soberly assessed the odds: five Frenchmen, fresh, well-fed and rested, to every Englishman, exhausted, pale and hungry.

'Oh that we now had here but one ten thousand of the men in England that do no work today!' wished the Earl of Westmoreland.

'No, my fair cousin,' cried the king, all marks of the night's heavy toil washed from him, standing firm and confident before them all, 'if we are marked to die, we are enough to give our country loss; and if to live, the fewer men, the greater share of honour! He that outlives this day and comes safe home, will stand on tip-toe when this day is named, and strip his sleeve and show his scars . . . This story shall the good man teach his son, and to the ending of the world, we in it shall be remembered, we few, we band of brothers; for he today that sheds his blood with me shall be my brother. All things are ready, if our minds be so!'

Ten thousand Frenchmen lost their lives that day at Agincourt, amongst them more than eight thousand princes, barons, lords, knights and squires . . . the young nobility of France.

In English ranks there were but twenty-five men dead. Though Ensign Pistol moved about the battlefield selling desperate Frenchmen their lives back for the rattle of a bag of gold, and went away well-pleased with the profitability of showing mercy, other men talked of how that day had brought forth all the honour, brotherhood and chivalry of brave men fighting side by side, and that this, against all reckoning of numbers, had won the day for Henry and his band of Englishmen. Weakened by hunger and exhaustion, shaken to the roots of their conviction by the fluttering banners of the vast host of Frenchmen who barred their path to safety, they had yet surged into battle with a lion's courage, winning all. And many men had cause to remember that young king, who had led them to the field of Agincourt, and led them out again, victorious.

From Agincourt, the army made their way, unhindered, to Calais and from there to England. But in time the return to France was needed. There, in the language of diplomacy much strengthened by the savage fist of war, a longer peace was sought, with satisfaction of the English claim to France's crown that would bring no further bloodshed and allow the French to rebuild their land, laid waste by nearly a century of recurring warfare. Her fields lay barren, her vineyards torn and trampled into mud, her soil untilled and overgrown with choking weeds, and the people whose lives should have laboured to create a richness on the land had all turned to the butchery of war, all other knowledge, learning, science, forgotten . . .

And so Henry returned to France. Amongst his demands for peace there was the hand of Katherine, the French king's daughter, in marriage. Bluntly he wooed her, with a soldier's humour, and a politician's tongue.

'It is not possible you should love the enemy of France,' he told her, 'but in loving me, you should love the friend of France; for I love France so well that I will not part with a village of it; I will have it all mine: and, Kate, when France is mine and I am yours, then yours is France and you are mine. Therefore tell me, most fair Katherine, will you have me? Take me by the hand and say "Harry of England I am yours", which word you shall no sooner bless my ear with, but I will tell you aloud, "England is yours, Ireland is yours, France is yours, and Henry is yours." Come,' he urged her with a grin, 'give me your answer in broken music, for your voice is music and your English is broken.'

Though the princess blushed modestly and deferred to the decision of her father, there was no doubt that Katherine's eyes shone bright for England's king. And when the king her father, granting all of Henry's demands, also gave her in marriage, both happiness and the bargain of peace were sealed: King Charles of France would remain as France's king until his death, and then to Henry and his heirs would go the throne of France. In the children of his marriage with the young princess, would also lie the unity between the rival kingdoms that faced each other so close across the sea.

The hope of peace that flowered in those days bloomed short. King Henry, who seemed to England's people to be their gleaming star, died young, and though his son, no more than three months old, was crowned the infant King of England and of France, there were other hands who ruled for him, and too many of them. New rivalries were bred, new arguments that festered in the kingdom's heart, and France was lost. England bled again in war and civil strife . . .

Richard the Third

King Henry V, the warrior-king of Agincourt was dead and his infant
son crowned Henry VI of England. For nearly forty years England was
to bleed in the savage turbulence of his son's reign.

He was a babe in arms when he became England's king, and so his
uncles ruled for him. Around them they grouped other lords who
wanted control of wealth and power. The great families of England
jostled to get closer to the royal seat: mighty lords became mightier,
their private armies larger and more lawless and their ambitions more
feverishly venomous . . .

The roots of the disorder lay in that year of 1399 when the king's
grandfather, Henry Bolingbroke, Duke of Lancaster, had seized the
crown from his own cousin Richard's head. By that act he usurped the
rightful line of kings which passed the crown from eldest son to eldest
son. Richard's father *was* the eldest son of King Edward III, but had
died young. Henry's father was no more than the third son. Yet Richard
was toppled from the throne and murdered, and Henry had the
crown.

He had thrown open the door to chaos: for more than eighty years the
decendants of Edward's many sons would fight each other for the prize
of England's crown.

It was during the reign of Henry VI, first infant king then boy-king,
then wed by the ruling lords to the strong-willed, ambitious French
princess Margaret of Anjou, that the rival parties swelled into two great
warring factions. On one side stood the family, supporters and the
private army of the House of York, who claimed their right to England's
throne from Edward III's second son.

On the other stood the House of Lancaster, the descendants of
Edward's third son, the Duke of Lancaster, father to King Henry IV.

For the moment, the great grandson of Henry IV, the Lancastrian King Henry VI, occupied the throne.

But he was unfitted for the reigns of power in such a vicious world, no more than a pawn in their game, used, abandoned, used, and again abandoned.

These were the Wars of the Roses, so-called because the House of York sported a white rose badge as it fought the red rose of the House of Lancaster. Through battle after battle they slaughtered one another, first Yorkists and then Lancastrians winning, until the young Duke of York emerged triumphant from the bloodiest battle of them all, at Towton. In the year 1461 he ascended to the throne as King Edward IV, deposed the Lancastrian Henry VI and sent him to prison in the Tower of London.

But there was still fight left in the House of Lancaster, and there was, as yet, no peace in England. Only ten years later on the battlefield at Tewkesbury, were the remnants of the Lancastrians all destroyed. At Tewkesbury the Lancastrian heir to the throne, son of Henry VI, was killed; swiftly afterwards, Henry VI was murdered in the Tower.

The House of York had always had the stronger claim to the crown than their Lancastrian cousins. With a Yorkist king now on the throne and the Lancastrian contenders mostly dead, England's people hoped for some return to peace. Generations had grown up without ever knowing their country unravaged by the butchery of war.

It seemed to everyone that the Yorkists were fair set for a settled reign: a handsome, popular king known to enjoy merriment and laughter, and with a son to inherit the throne for him. Could anything disturb the peaceful progress of these times?

This was the question pondered by the king's youngest brother, Richard Duke of Gloucester, as he limped along a London street in the melancholy light of a waning afternoon, his dark, hunched figure plunging in and out of lengthening shadows. There was a half-smile on his face, a grin it might be called, though such a thin-lipped twist did not inspire so jovial a name, nor did the deep-hidden glimmers of his narrowed eyes. They roamed ceaselessly across the picture of the tall, easy king and his pretty queen which Richard carried ever-present in his mind, though not for love. 'Now is the winter of our discontent made glorious summer by this sun of York,' he murmured, and the words were light with scorn, yet dark with other echoes . . .

He paused, and allowed his thoughts to stray across the memory of Tewkesbury and other battlefields, in years gone by. He saw again the broken savagery of dead that strewed those fields, but it was a vision he viewed calmly, almost curiously, without emotion now. It was all over. 'All the clouds that loured upon our house are in the deep bosom of the ocean buried,' he said. 'Now are our brows bound with victorious wreathes, our bruised arms hung up for monuments, our stern alarms changed to merry meetings, our dreadful marches to delightful dances. Grim-visaged war has smoothed his wrinkled brow, and now he capers nimbly in a lady's chamber to the lascivious pleasing of a lute!'

He fell to silence, considering again the elegance of the gracious king and pretty queen, and they were not thoughts he liked. 'But I,' he said, 'I, that am not shaped for sportive tricks, I, deformed, unfinished, sent before my time into this breathing world scarce half made up, I am determined to prove a villain and hate the idle pleasure of these days.' The comment, coldly made, seeded a gleam of fire in Richard's voice, and he thought with sudden pleasure of his plots, new-laid, to set his elder brother Clarence and the king against each other . . . He had told the king of a prophecy that his heirs would be murdered by someone with a name beginning with the letter G!

This mischievous thought was interrupted by the arrival in the street of Clarence himself, close-guarded and accompanied by the warden of the Tower of London. Now was Richard's inward musing look swiftly exchanged for the sharp concern of loving brother for his brother's plight. He hurried forward. 'What means this armed guard that waits upon your grace?' he demanded anxiously.

The Duke of Clarence shook his head, despair dulling any other thought. The king, it seemed, had ordered him into the Tower. Why? Because his first name, George, began with G . . .

Richard's smile of glee was thinly masked beneath the veil of brotherly concern. 'It is not the king that sends you to the Tower; it is his wife, the queen, it is she that pushes him to this extremity,' he exclaimed. 'We are not safe, Clarence; we are not safe,' he shook his head with sorrow, 'Well,' he clapped his brother on the shoulder, jovial, encouraging, 'Your imprisonment shall not be long. I will deliver you. Meantime, have patience.'

His brother's dejected figure flanked by guards moved out of sight. 'Simple, plain Clarence!' whispered Richard after him, 'I do love you so, that I will shortly send your soul to heaven!' He savoured this, and moved on towards the palace. A figure came along the street towards him, carrying news of some import: it seemed the king had fallen sick, was growing weaker by the hour, his doctors much afraid for him . . .

Richard brooded on this new turn to events. With luck, the king would die. But not, he hoped, before plain Clarence could be packed towards the heavens. 'I'll go in,' he resolved, 'and urge his hatred more to Clarence, with lies well steeled with weighty arguments . . .' With luck, and much hard work by Richard, Clarence would not have another day to live! 'Which done, God take King Edward to his mercy, and leave the world for me to bustle in,' said Richard merrily.

Then he would marry the grieving widow, Anne. This lady Anne was the wife of King Henry VI's son, the Lancastrian heir to the throne, killed by Richard on the battlefield of Tewkesbury. Soon after he had also killed his father, Henry VI, immured in the Tower.

What did it matter if he had killed both Lady Anne's husband and her father-in-law? What better way to make amends than to provide her with a new husband, himself? Much enlivened by these warming prospects, Richard and his shadow limped like two dark birds of prey towards the palace.

The corpse of Henry VI being carried along the street, guarded, had but a single mourner. She walked slowly, in a trance, tears falling silently across ashen cheeks.

'Poor key-cold figure of a holy king!' she whispered. 'Pale ashes of the house of Lancaster! You bloodless remnant of that royal blood!' She stared with hollow eyes beyond the pitiful shrunken figure of dead Henry, once a king, into a world of infinite misery, 'Be it lawful that I call up your ghost to hear the lamentations of poor Anne, wife to your slaughtered son, stabbed by the self-same hand that made these wounds,' she wept, and suddenly she was bending low across the body of the murdered king, 'Cursed be the hand that made these fatal holes! Cursed be the heart that had the heart to do it! Cursed be the blood that let this blood flow! If ever he have wife, let her be made as miserable by the death of him as I am made by my poor lord and you!'

She looked up as a shadow fell across the corpse and caught her in its lingering gloom. The object of her curse had stepped across their path and barred their onward movement. She stared trembling at the man whose sword had widowed her. Richard, Duke of Gloucester, eyed her calmly.

'Foul devil,' she hissed, 'if you delight to see your hideous deeds, behold this pattern of your butcheries. Blush, blush, you lump of foul deformity,' she cried, scarce able to look upon his hated face.

'Lady,' interrupted Richard, 'you know no rules of charity, which offers good for bad, blessings for curses.'

'Villain,' Anne sobbed, disgust contorting the misery of her young face into a fire of hatred, 'you know no law of God or man! There is no beast so fierce that does not know some touch of pity.'

'But I know none,' Richard said with a smile, 'and therefore am no beast.'

She stared in disbelief at his mocking face unmoved by all the hatred she could pour on it.

'Gentle Lady Anne,' Richard smiled on, 'Your beauty was the cause . . . Your beauty, which did haunt me in my sleep to undertake the death of all the world so I might live one hour in your sweet bosom.'

All colour fled from the young widow's face. 'If I thought that, these nails would tear that beauty from my cheeks!' she vowed.

'He that deprived you, lady, of a husband, did it to help you to a better husband!' said Richard unperturbed.

She glowered as if she longed to kill him where he stood, and all the fury of her pent-up misery gathered like a storm, and suddenly she spat, full in his smiling face.

The smile left it. 'Why do you spit at me?' he asked.

'Out of my sight,' she cried, 'you do infect my eyes.'

'Your eyes, sweet lady, have infected mine,' he rejoined, for he was going to net his quarry, spit or no. 'Teach not your lips such scorn, for they were made for kissing lady, not for such contempt.' And suddenly he dropped to his knees, ripped back his shirt to bare his chest, offering his sword to her, 'If your revengeful heart cannot forgive, here I lend you this sharp-pointed sword! I lay my bosom naked to the deadly stroke and humbly beg the death upon my knee! I did kill King Henry, but it was your beauty that provoked me! It was I that stabbed his son, your husband, but it was your heavenly face that set me on!'

She seized the sword in passionate hatred, and made to plunge it in

his heart. But then a moment later she let it fall again, unused. She
turned away, the fever of the moment lost in the plunge to blackest
misery.

'Take up the sword again,' warned Richard, 'or take up me.'

'Arise, dissembler,' the widow Anne replied, 'though I wish your
death, I will not be your executioner.'

'Then bid me kill myself, and I will do it,' said Richard, exulting in
his power already winding over her.

'I have already,' she answered wearily.

'That was in your rage. Speak it again, and even with your word, this
hand, which for your love did kill your love, shall kill a far truer love,'
he leapt into his lies of passion with the gusto of a man who knew that he
was drawing near his goal.

She stared wanly at him, fury and misery drowning in confusion. 'I
wish I knew your heart,' she murmured, lost in the web of words he
spun about her exhausted brain. She knew every word was false, but
she had ceased to have the strength to move away.

'But shall I live in hope?' pressed Richard, much enjoying this role of ardent wooer.

'All men I hope, live so,' she answered, barely hearing him.

He seized her hand, and pressed a ring upon her finger, and in a trance she moved away from him, all passion spent, all opposition dulled.

Pleasure danced across Richard's lips in a smile of scorn. 'I'll have her,' he nodded to himself, 'but I will not keep her long.'

The queen paced anxiously: the king's illness was worsening, and more than fear for his life clouded her thoughts. What would become of her, once he was dead? His marriage to her was not welcomed by the most powerful lords; she was the widow and the sister of Lancastrians, and her family was not among the powerful. But Edward had been obstinate and he had married her, swiftly showering wealth and favours on her sons and brothers, but giving birth to envy amongst the lords of England, envy which was barely kept in check. If King Edward were to die, she did not doubt that envy would break through its restraining bonds.

And if Edward were to die and their young son be crowned as king, the years before he was old enough to rule himself had been put into the hand of Richard Duke of Gloucester, a man whose eyes smoked hatred for her and all her family . . . She felt no comfort in the knowledge that the king, feeling the approach of death, had sent for all of them to reconcile themselves to one another.

Richard, ever energetic in the pursuance of his master plot, was even now hurling accusations at her: she had, he claimed, caused the imprisonment of Clarence! Tearfully, fear giving way to indignation, the queen denied all hand in it, as well she might, being entirely innocent of anything but the most earnest pleas for Clarence's release.

But even the venom of their argument could not reach the poison spewed at them by Queen Margaret, the furious widow of the dead Henry VI. She came upon them quarrelling and watched them with a deadly hatred. 'Hear me, you wrangling pirates, that fall out in sharing that which you have taken from me! A husband and a son you owe to me,' she hissed at Richard. Richard returned the venom of her look, for this was the Lancastrian queen who had killed his father on the battlefield at Wakefield and fixed his severed head high on the gate at York.

Margaret rounded on the tearful queen of Edward, 'And *you* owe me a kingdom. Let Edward, your son, who is now Prince of Wales, for Edward my son, who was the Prince of Wales, die in his youth by like untimely violence! Yourself a queen, for me that was a queen, outlive your glory, like my wretched self! Long may you live to wail your children's loss, and see another, as I see you now, decked in your rights as you are installed in mine. Long die your happy days before your death, and, after many lengthened hours of grief die neither as mother, wife, nor England's queen!'

'Have done with your charm, you hateful withered hag,' snarled Richard.

'And leave you out?' she cried. She rounded on him then, her face contorted with disgust. 'The worm of conscience shall begnaw your soul! You shall suspect your friends as traitors while you live and take deep traitors for your dearest friends! No sleep close up that deadly eye of yours, unless it be whilst some tormenting dream affrights you with the hell of ugly devils!'

And to the Duke of Buckingham, she turned and hissed. 'Oh, Buckingham, take heed of yonder dog! Look, when he fawns, he bites, and when he bites his venom tooth will rankle to the death: have not to do with him, beware of him; sin, death and hell have set their marks on him . . .'

'What does she say?' asked Richard curiously.

'Nothing that I respect, my gracious lord,' said Buckingham, and stood with Richard, watching Margaret sweep from the room, still spitting fury.

'My hair stands up on end to hear her curses,' the Lord Hastings commented.

'I cannot blame her,' Richard said, 'she has suffered too much wrong, and I repent my part in it . . .'

His plot proceeded with all speed: even as he bewailed the imprisonment of Clarence, and convinced the Lords of Hastings, Buckingham and Stanley that it was the queen and her family who were the cause of it, he despatched two murderers to put paid to Clarence in the Tower.

The Duke of Clarence, plunged from the sunlit place beside the king at Court into the dank gloom of the Tower, was gripped by torturing dreams of dark foreboding. 'I thought that I had broken from the Tower,' he told the warden, 'and was embarked to sail across to France. And in my company, my brother Richard tempted me to walk upon the hatches; we looked towards England, and talked of a thousand fearful times during the wars of York and Lancaster that had befallen us. As we paced along upon the giddy footing of the hatches, I thought that Richard stumbled, and in falling struck me overboard into the tumbling billows of the main.' He trembled, wiping his hand across his eyes, and stared again into the horror of the dream, 'Lord, lord, I thought, what pain it was to drown, what dreadful noise of waters in my ears! I thought I saw a thousand fearful wrecks; ten thousand men that fishes gnawed upon, wedges of gold, great anchors, heaps of pearls, unvalued jewels . . . some lay in dead men's skulls . . .' and how he had tried to die and escape that pounding depth!

When he slept again, they came, those murderers of brother Richard, with daggers bought with gold, and stopped his cries for mercy by

plunging him head-first into a cask of wine, to drown, as he had
dreamed he would . . .

The dying king sought reconciliation between his queen and those
among the lords who had set themselves against her. To allay his fears,
they pledged peace and friendship as he asked. First Lord Hastings: his
opposition to the queen and family had led to his imprisonment in the
Tower from which he was just now released; he swore loyalty to the
queen, her sons and brothers, and they to him. Then the Duke of
Buckingham pledged the same.

Richard, absent from these warming ceremonies, but choosing to
arrive most aptly as the bonds were sworn, entered with full flowing
poetry into the swearing of his loyalty to all. 'If any here hold me a foe,'
he cried, 'I desire to reconcile me to his friendly peace. It is death to me
to be at enmity, I hate it and desire all good men's love!' Then first of
the queen, and then of Buckingham, then of the queen's brother Lord
Rivers and her son Lord Grey, he asked for pardon for any ills. 'Dukes,
earls, lords, gentlemen,' he encompassed all of them in his happy smile,
'I do not know that Englishman alive with whom my soul is any jot at
odds more than the infant that is born tonight!'

The queen, in relief at such happy words, added her plea to the king
to embrace imprisoned Clarence in this hour of forgiveness. Richard
rounded on her, black with rage. She was mocking him! She, of all
must know the Duke of Clarence was already dead!

The news struck like a dagger through their smiles, and left them
ragged, pale and lifeless. All stared at one another, seeking guilt on
others' faces.

'Is Clarence dead?' the failing king gasped out, 'the order was
reversed!'

'How the guilty kindred of the queen looked pale when they did hear
of Clarence's death!' Richard murmured in the ear of Buckingham.
'Oh, they did urge it on the king! God will revenge it,' he said with
pious certainty.

King Edward, grieving for his brother Clarence, died, and thoughts
turned to the heir to England's crown, his son, the boy Edward, Prince
of Wales, who must now be brought to London to be crowned as king.

'My lord,' Buckingham spoke now in Richard's ear, 'whoever journeys to the prince, for God's sake, let not us two be behind,' for Buckingham's sharp eyes had seen the way the stream of power was flowing and knew it would shortly gather flood: he, of all, was going to ride its current to high tide.

'My other self, my oracle, my prophet!' Richard applauded him. 'My dear cousin, I, like a child, will go by your direction!'

And so they went to Ludlow to fetch the king-to-be. In London the queen waited eagerly to see her son, her shifting fears calmed by the pleasure that the lords had chosen to bring him for coronation. But even as she waited, news came that her brother Lord Rivers and her son Lord Grey had been immured in Pomfret Castle, prisoners, and by the orders of the Dukes of Buckingham and Gloucester.

It had begun. 'Aye me,' she wept, 'I see the downfall of our house! The tiger has now seized the gentle deer; insulting tyranny begins to strut upon the innocent and aweless throne! Welcome, destruction, death and massacre! I see, as in a map, the end of all!'

And so it had begun again: blood against blood, self against self; treachery and murder for a kingdom and a crown.

The queen fled to the protection of the Church, to sanctuary, and took her youngest son with her, her mother's heart filled with terror for her eldest son, Edward, Prince of Wales, just twelve years old, who rode to London with his uncle Richard and his uncle's friend, the Duke of Buckingham.

'Welcome, sweet prince, to London,' Buckingham hailed the king-to-be, and trumpets peeled to welcome the heir to England's royal throne.

'Welcome, dear cousin,' smiled his uncle Richard. 'The weary way has made you melancholy,' he said, with soft concern.

'No uncle, but I want more uncles here to welcome me,' the boy prince said, thinking of his missing uncles Rivers and the Duke of Clarence.

'Sweet prince,' said Richard with a smile, 'the untainted virtue of your years has not yet dived into the world's deceit. Those uncles which you want were dangerous: Your Grace attended to their sugared words, but looked not on the poison of their hearts: God keep you from them and from such false friends!'

'God keep me from false friends!' the prince echoed the words, 'but they were none,' he said defiantly.

The eager home-coming was to prove more dismal still: no mother and no younger brother either; both had taken sanctuary. And he must stay, until his coronation, in the Tower.

'I do not like the Tower,' the prince protested, though these thoughts were for the moment swept away by the arrival of his younger brother, plucked by force from his mother's arms in sanctuary to come and greet him, and running eager to his older brother's arms, more interested in who had grown the most since last they met, than with deadly currents of power that the older boy, so young, could sense.

'My lord, will it please you pass along?' Richard interrupted them. 'Myself and my good cousin Buckingham will go to your mother, to entreat her to meet you at the Tower and welcome you.'

The little prince looked pale, 'I shall not sleep quiet at the Tower. I fear my uncle Clarence's angry ghost: my grandmother told me he was murdered there!'

'I fear no uncles dead,' said the Prince of Wales, with a grimness in his voice that was beyond his years.

'Nor none that live, I hope,' said Richard, with a smile.

'If they live, I hope I need not fear,' the heir to England's throne replied, and with a heavy heart he took his little brother's hand, and went towards the Tower.

Richard and Buckingham began to stretch their net a little wider. Into their cause they must draw all who might advance Richard's clamber to the throne. Sir William Catesby was already one with them and his services could be relied upon to test out others: first, could Lord Hastings be persuaded to help install Richard in the royal seat of England?

Catesby thought not, for Hastings loved the young heir to the throne for dead King Edward's sake. And what of Lord Stanley, often in Lord Hastings' company?

'He will do all as Hastings does,' said Catesby.

Hastings must be tried at least, said Buckingham: he should be sounded out and brought to London to discuss the coronation of the Prince of Wales. And as enticement for his interest in their cause, Richard added, he must be told that his enemies, the queen's brother

and son, would be put to death tomorrow at Pomfret Castle. 'And bid
my friend, for joy of this good news, give Mistress Shore one gentle kiss
the more,' said Richard, naming the well-known lady who was
Hastings' lover.

Catesby sped away to fulfil his orders.

'Now, my lord,' asked Buckingham of Richard, 'what shall we do if
we perceive Lord Hastings will not join our plot?'

'Chop off his head, man,' came the jovial reply from Richard. But
seeing Buckingham's somewhat startled look, he laughed again, and
clapped him on the back, 'And look, when I am king, claim from me
the earldom of Hereford, and look to have it yielded with all
willingness . . .'

Another messenger reached Lord Hastings first, sent by his friend Lord
Stanley. He sent word that he had dreamed that night that Richard
turned on both of them, as he had already turned on Lord Rivers and
Lord Grey. He urged that both of them should ride towards the north at
once, to escape the danger.

But Hastings was bursting with good-humoured confidence. No
danger could be threatening, and they would both be well-informed of
any brewing, for would not Hastings' servant, Catesby, bring him news
of it? On that note he greeted Catesby, arriving with the tasks set him by
Richard.

'What news, what news in this our tottering state?' he asked.

'It is a reeling world, indeed, my lord,' answered Catesby carefully,
'and I believe it will never stand upright till Richard wear the garland of
the realm.'

'How! Wear the garland! Do you mean the crown?' said Hastings
sharply. 'I'll have this crown of mine cut from my shoulders before I
will see the crown so foul misplaced! But do you guess that he does aim
at it?' he asked, surprised.

'Ay, on my life,' Catesby confirmed, 'and hopes to find you joining
with his party for that gain; and thereupon he sends you this good news,
that this same day your enemies, the kindred of the queen, must die at
Pomfret.'

Hastings shook his head. That news was good, for they had all been
bitter enemies, but to help lift Richard to the throne, and bar King
Edward's heirs in true descent! 'God knows I will not do it, to the

death,' he cried, and did not know he'd thereby signed his death warrant, and that this signature would be carried swift to Richard by his own, trusted, Catesby.

At the council with the other lords to discuss the coronation, he sat unsuspecting, commenting with good humour on how jovial Richard looked today.

'I think there is no man can less hide his love or hate than he, for by his face straight shall you know his heart,' he said.

'What of his heart do you read in his face today?' asked Stanley whose ominous dream still preyed upon his mind.

'Why, that with no man here is he offended, for if he were, he would show it in his looks,' said Hastings, and he turned with all of them to greet Richard, who entered fast, as though deep in thought upon some distant problem.

'I pray you all, tell me what they deserve that do conspire my death with devilish plots of damned witchcraft, and that have prevailed upon my body with their hellish charms,' he asked, and looked at Hastings.

Startled, Hastings said, 'My lord, they have deserved death.'

'Then be your eyes the witness of this ill,' snarled Richard, 'see how I am bewitched; behold my arm is, like a blasted sapling, withered up. And this is Edward's wife, the queen, that monstrous witch, consorted with that harlot strumpet Shore, that by their witchcraft thus have marked me!' And with an avenging fury he flung the twisted arm out at white-faced Hastings. 'You damned protector of this Shore, you are a traitor: off with his head! Lovell and Ratcliff, look that it be done!'

And with a yell of fury Richard flung from the room, the lords all leaving with him, and only Lovell and Ratcliff ranked on either side of Hastings.

Hastings, half-risen from his seat in shock, sank back again. He knew he was already dead, he, who in his blind self-confidence had thrust all warnings off. 'Miserable England!' he whispered. 'I prophesy the fearfullest time for you that ever wretched age has looked upon!' He looked up, and met the impatient eyes of Lovell and Ratcliff, who had work to do.

They brought Hastings' head to Richard as he talked with the Lord Mayor of London. Richard bent a sorrowful eye on it, and wiped his hand across his eyes as though to hide a tear. 'So dear I loved the man,' he sighed, 'that I must weep. I took him for the plainest harmless creature that breathed upon this earth. So smooth he daubed his vice with show of virtue!'

'We live to tell it to you, the subtle traitor this day had plotted, in the council-house to murder me and my good Lord of Gloucester!' added Buckingham, for good measure.

So, with lies and savage conspiracy did Richard and the Duke of Buckingham begin their final climb towards the throne. Some men believed their lies, some wished not to know the truth, and others trembled in their fear . . .

Richard's plot unfolded further: the next task must be to let the people know that Edward's sons, the princes in the Tower were not the sons of Edward by his wife, the queen, but by some other woman, and were not entitled to the crown of England . . .

Buckingham hurried off to put this news about. Richard prepared to receive the restless crowd of people raised to condemn the accession of the Prince of Wales to England's throne and raise the cry for Richard as their king.

It was not an easy task, and Buckingham returned frustrated. He had done all as planned, thrown slander on the dead king's name, claimed that the princes were not true heirs to the crown, and when he'd ended with the cry of 'God save Richard, England's royal king!' there had not been a single voice to echo it.

A performance of some care was needed to draw out this clamour for Richard to be king. Carefully they all prepared it: the Mayor with citizens was brought to Richard's castle to speak with him. Richard let it be known that he was locked in prayer with two bishops, the very picture of devotion to the worship of God and the opposite of the lascivious dead King Edward, he who spawned sons out of wedlock with no care for England's health!

Every detail was finished with some care: Richard, unwilling to be disturbed from devout meditations; the citizens brought there by Buckingham; Catesby running to and fro as though from Buckingham to Richard, still piously at his devotions, to bring word he could not be disturbed and would not talk to them; Buckingham pleading for an audience; Richard, appearing on the balcony locked fast in prayer, and interrupted with some difficulty from his meditation, to hear the petition from the people so eloquently delivered for them by the Duke of Buckingham. It was Richard's duty and his right, the right of England to demand that he take up his place upon the throne, and push aside the unlawful sons of Edward!

The listening Richard frowned; he thanked them for their love, but he was unworthy of so high an office as the throne of England, and there were rightful heirs . . .

Not so, cried earnest Buckingham; and played the tune again of Edward's lewdness, his unlawful sons from women other than the queen. The troubled Richard clutched his prayer-book tighter to his bosom and took on a look of sorrow, but would not yield, so filled was he with his unworthiness to be king.

They pleaded with him: Catesby, Buckingham, and then the Mayor, and then one by one, the citizens . . .

Reluctantly, he listened to their pleas; unwillingly he bowed his

head. The burden placed on him by the love and loyalty of all the people must be lifted up and carried, painful and weighty though it might be: he must be king, if they so wanted it, and he, (though he did not wish it for a moment), must bow to their demand.

'Then I salute you with this kingly title: long live Richard, England's royal king!' cried Buckingham. 'Tomorrow, will it please you to be crowned?'

'Even when it please, since you will have it so,' said Richard, deferring to the people's wishes, and returning to his holy task of prayer.

And so Richard Duke of Gloucester was crowned King Richard III of England, and by his side the Lady Anne, who had once spat her hatred in his face and cursed him for the murder of her husband, but who swayed at the skilful honey-winding of his tongue, and married him, and for her pains had reaped the bitter harvest of her own fierce curse. She knew as she watched the gathering pace of tyranny around her, that this king would shortly be rid of her.

The princes in the Tower were now imprisoned, mother, grandmother and aunts all barred from seeing them. Their half-brother, Lord Dorset fled across the sea to Britanny, where Lord Stanley's step-son, Henry Tudor, Earl of Richmond, and the next Lancastrian heir to the throne, lived in exile and would welcome him.

King Richard sat upon the throne and eyed Buckingham. One question needed answering: would he wear these honours merely for a day; or would they last?

'Young Edward lives,' said Richard, 'think now what I would say,' he urged, and looked at Buckingham again.

'Say on, my loving lord,' said Buckingham.

'Why, Buckingham, I say I would be king!' repeated Richard.

'Why so you are, my thrice renowned liege,' nodded Buckingham.

'But Edward lives.'

'True, noble prince,' acknowledged Buckingham, refusing to understand the king.

'Cousin,' said Richard harshly, 'you did not used to be so dull. Shall I be plain? I wish the bastards dead. What do you say? Speak suddenly: be brief!'

There was a pause, and Buckingham eyed the king, and in that look there was a wealth of meaning.

'Say,' hissed Richard, 'have I your consent that they shall die?'

'Give me some breath, some little pause, my lord, before I positively answer this,' said Buckingham quietly, and bowing, he withdrew.

But Richard had his answer, and it was enough for him: thus far had Buckingham come with him, but now he hesitated, and for that moment's hesitation he would be allowed to go no further.

He gave orders: first, quietly to his page, to find a man who would dare a dangerous exploit for payment in gold; second, to the ever-faithful Catesby, instructions to put out rumours that Anne, his wife, was sick, and likely to die. Richard had a new plan afoot: to marry his brother Edward's daughter. Murder her brothers, and then marry her! 'But I am in so far in blood that sin will pluck on sin,' he mused, 'tear-falling pity dwells not in this eye.'

And now the final orders, the last stage of his plan, swift instructions to the man brought by his page: kill the princes in the Tower.

With these orders given, he stared past Buckingham, when he returned. He would not hear him. Buckingham had come to ask a question: what of that earldom of Hereford once promised him by Richard?

'I am not in the giving vein today,' said Richard, and brushed him off.

Now Buckingham understood: he thought of Hastings, dead, and knew that he must flee at once to safety, while his own head still sat securely on his shoulders.

Richard heard that Lord Dorset had fled to the Earl of Richmond in Britanny. He did not like the news, nor did he like the name of Richmond. He had been told once, by a bard of Ireland, that he would not live long after he saw Richmond, and had thought till now that meant a place . . .

The princes in the Tower, their young arms cradling each other, their faces smooth in innocence upon a pillow where a book of prayer lay open, slept on and did not stir as King Richard's murderers entered the room. Their bodies, limp and pale, were hurried secretly away and buried, and now it seemed that Richard sat in safety on his stolen throne.

Richard heard the news with relish, and counted up the other measures taken: the Duke of Clarence's son was now in prison, Anne, Richard's wife was dead, and now that Richard knew that the Earl of Richmond was suitor for dead King Edward's daughter's hand, he knew that his next task must be to marry her himself, and so secure the crown.

But suddenly all did not look so smooth: a clutch of lords had gone to the Earl of Richmond, to ask him to come and take the crown; and Buckingham had fled to raise an army backed with hardy Welshmen . . .

'Come, muster men,' King Richard cried, 'we must be brief when traitors brave the field!'

Richmond had crossed the Channel and was nearing England's western shores; there people flocked to greet him; every hour news came to King Richard of more and more. And it was said that, urged on by the lords who'd fled to him from Richard's tyranny, Richmond had come to take the crown.

'Is the chair empty? Is the sword unswayed? Is the king dead? the empire unpossessed?' yelled Richard. 'What heir of York is there alive but we? And who is England's king but great York's heir?'

He rounded on the Earl of Stanley furiously, for this man was the Earl of Richmond's step-father. 'I will not trust you sir,' he said. 'Go, muster men, but hear you, leave behind your son, George Stanley. Let your faith be firm to me, or else his head's security will be but frail!'

And still the messengers came flying in; to north and west the lords were mustering arms against Richard.

'Away, towards Salisbury!' cried Richard. 'While we reason here a royal battle might be won and lost.'

His last remaining loyalty cut from him by the seizure of his son, Stanley sent secret word to Richmond: he could not openly show his support for fear of his son's life, but his heart and arms would be for Richmond. And he sent other news, news that would win many hands to Richmond's cause: dead Edward's queen had consented that Richmond should marry her daughter, Elizabeth of York: so would a Lancastrian be united with the House of York and bring an end to the savage war for England's crown.

Near Leicester, Richard mustered forces for the battle. Henry Tudor, Earl of Richmond, gathered supporters as he came and urged those who flocked to him to reap the harvest of perpetual peace by this one bloody trial of war against a tyrant.

On Bosworth field the two armies camped: Richard's army, uneasy, seething with shifting loyalties, weary with the bloodshed and conspiracy that filled his reign, and Henry Earl of Richmond, with only some five thousand men, but strong with the will to end the blood of Richard's reign and find a peace for England.

Henry from his tent watched the golden sunset fade and a raw, cold night set in. He gave his final orders for the night. At dawn the battle would begin, and in the meantime final plans must be discussed, the lines of battle drawn, and secret messages sent out across the field to Stanley . . .

Richard paced inside his tent, giving orders: ink and paper! His armour, was it ready? Had a Watch been mounted with full care, with trusty sentinels? His lances were all sound? And tell Lord Stanley that he must bring his army up before sunrise lest his son George fall into the blind cave of eternal night . . .

Across the field, in Richmond's tent, the Earl of Stanley spoke in secret with his step-son, and pledged that though he would remain with Richard till the battled started, on that instant would he fight for Richmond's cause.

And so the king who wore the stolen crown, and the earl who came to wrestle it from him, each settled in their tents, to rest before the dawn would bring the battle for the crown.

For Richard there would be no rest: they came for him, the ghosts of all he'd murdered for the crown. They marched in menacing array across the night's raw air, and echoed in his head, and gathered in their bloody rags about his bed, and through the night their curses whispered, shimmered on and on and on: the dead Lancastrian king and prince, the Duke of Clarence, the ghosts of Rivers, Grey, the shaking head of Hastings, the two princes in the Tower, the ghost of Anne, his wife, the ghost of Buckingham, now captured and

beheaded . . . on and on and on they came, 'Despair and die!' they shrilled, 'Tomorrow in the battle, think on me, despair and die . . .'

But to the sleeping Earl of Richmond the souls of Richard's dead sent blessings, 'Good angels guide your battle, live and flourish. Awake, arm, fight and conquer, for fair England's sake! Live and beget a happy race of kings,' their echo faded in the dawn.

In terror Richard started up, his body dank with icy sweat, and knowledge black within him of his guilt, his poisoning hatred towards all, 'There is no creature loves me; and if I die, no soul shall pity me,' he cried. 'Nay, why should they, since I myself find in myself no pity for myself?'

Across the field, Richmond woke with thoughts of victory warm in his heart: it seemed to him that in the night he'd heard the souls of all of Richard's dead cry out to him and wish him victory.

'Remember this,' he hailed his soldiers, 'God and our good cause fight on our side, the prayers of holy saints and wronged souls stand before our faces; those whom we fight would rather have us win than him they follow; for what is he but a tyrant raised in blood, and one in blood established, who slaughtered those that were the means to help him!'

'Remember whom you fight,' across the field of Bosworth King Richard told his army. 'A sort of vagabonds,' he sneered, 'rascals and runaways, a scum of Bretons and base lackey peasant, whom their country vomits forth to desperate ventures and assured destruction. Let's whip these stragglers over the seas again. Shall they enjoy our lands? Hark, I hear the drum. Fight, gentlemen of England fight!'

'A horse! a horse! My kingdom for a horse!' Richard's cry rose in fury across the battlefield, while Catesby, ever faithful, yelled for rescue for the king.

'His horse is slain, and all on foot he fights, seeking for Richmond in the throat of death!' Catesby begged for help.

But treachery, that coin of Richard, now paid him for his infamy. Even as the battle had begun, a half his army had deserted him. Richard, still fighting with a demon fury, fell to Richmond's sword, as had been certain since the light of dawn had chased the shades of ghosts across the bare uplands of Bosworth field.

'God and your arms be praised, victorious friends,' the Earl of

Richmond gave heartfelt thanks. 'The day is ours. We will unite the white rose and the red: England has long been mad and scarred herself, the brother blindly shed the brother's blood, the father rashly slaughtered his own son . . . all this divided York and Lancaster. But now, let Richmond and Elizabeth, the true succeeders of each royal house, join, and let their heirs enrich the time to come with smooth-faced peace, with smiling plenty and fair prosperous days!'

So ended the bloody reign of Richard; so ended the wars between Lancaster and York. Henry, Earl of Richmond, descended from Lancastrians, married Elizabeth of York, and ascended to the throne of England as King Henry VII. The time of peace on England's soil had come at last.

The
Roman Histories

Julius Caesar

Rome awaited the mighty Caesar, its streets and bustling squares
seething with citizens eager to hail a leader's triumph. And Caesar was
no ordinary leader. He had defeated the rival general Pompey. He had
fought off the threat to his supremacy from Pompey's sons. Now Julius
Caesar held undisputed sway in Rome: dictator for life, commander of
the Roman army, the most powerful man in all the ancient world. He
ruled unchallenged.

But there were those in Rome who did not celebrate. They mourned
great Pompey's loss and loathed to see the people who rejoiced at
Pompey passing through the city applauding now at Caesar's triumph
over Pompey's blood. Decked out in holiday clothes, Rome's people
poured into the streets to strew the ground with flowers and decorate
the statues in Julius Caesar's honour.

It seemed the citizens of Rome were ripe to applaud any leader's
triumph . . .

Into the streets strode Caesar, flanked by smiling senators and borne
along amidst a jubilant mob of people, to shouts and cries of merriment
and trumpets heralding the running race through Rome in celebration
of this feast day.

The runners poised to begin. Caesar gave the signal. There was a
joyful flourish from the trumpets.

'Caesar!' a voice shrilled above the trumpet's song. 'Caesar!'

Caesar paused. 'Who calls? I hear a tongue cry "Caesar!" Speak,
Caesar is turned to hear.'

Again the wailing cry, shriller than any trumpet's note, 'Beware the
Ides of March . . .'

'What man is that?' demanded Caesar. 'Set him before me; let me see
his face.'

A flurry of activity amongst the crowd: a man fell forwards, stumbling before the dictator. He was old, and bent, and lined. He raised his eyes to Caesar's, and in them was the haunted look of one who gazed painfully into the future and read the fates of men.

'Speak once again!' commanded Caesar.

'Beware the Ides of March!' the old man's cry pierced the restless hubbub of the crowd . . . and suddenly there was a hush. The Ides of March: the fifteenth day of March. Today was already the first day of that month! Now all were watching.

The silence grew, a creeping chill across the day's bright warmth.

All waited. Caesar stared into the crumpled parchment of the old man's face.

And then he turned his back, 'He is a dreamer; let us leave him: pass.' Within a moment Caesar had swept on leaving the old man swallowed in the crowd which surged after the dictator along the narrow streets, even more buoyant on the wings of merriment than before, and eager for the celebration games.

There was one senator who lingered behind the departing crowd with other thoughts to occupy his mind. With saddened eyes he watched the progress of this mighty leader along the clamorous street. Brutus mourned Caesar's rise to power as he might mourn a death: but it was not in sadness at Pompey's loss.

Brutus loathed the rise to power of any single man: it was, he believed, the death of liberty. He dreamed of a glorious state of Rome ruled not by the whims and choices of a single, all-powerful man, but by the balanced wisdom of a collective senate. As he watched Julius Caesar stride from triumph to triumph as though nothing was strong enough to block his way, there was a twisting unease that clouded all of Brutus' waking hours; with the unease had come other thoughts that sat painfully within his mind, thoughts he almost dared not recognize . . .

As he wrestled with his thoughts, he too was watched, as carefully as he himself watched Caesar. His friend Cassius had seen Brutus's brooding mood and knew what troubled him.

A sudden shout and the triumphant peel of trumpets reached them. Brutus started, stung from his reverie. 'What does this shouting mean? I do fear the people choose Caesar for their king.'

'Aye, do you fear it?' murmured Cassius, moving closer. He paused, then said with care, 'Then must I think you would not have it so.'

'I would not, Cassius,' Brutus answered quietly, and sighed. 'Yet I love him well.' He looked along the street towards the clamour, as though he was again debating inwardly some painful course. And then he shook the thoughts away and turned to Cassius. He looked at him curiously, as though aware for the first time of the deliberate pattern of his friend's probing words.

'What is it that you would impart to me? If it be anything towards the general good, set honour in one eye and death in the other, and I will look on both indifferently: for I love the name of honour more than I fear death.'

'Well, honour is the subject of my story,' said Cassius. 'I cannot tell what you and other men think of this life, but for myself, I would as soon not be, as live to be in awe of such a thing as I myself!' He moved in front of Brutus to bar his onward movement along the street and force his close attention. 'I was born as free as Caesar; so were you: we both have fed as well, and we can both endure the winter's cold as well as he!' His eyes glittered and his voice grew sharp with scorn. 'And this man has now become a god, and Cassius is a wretched creature and must bend his body if Caesar carelessly nods to him . . .'

'Another general shout,' gasped Brutus, turning towards the distant uproar. 'I do believe that this applause is for some new honours that are heaped on Caesar!'

'Why, man,' Cassius burst out, 'he bestrides the narrow world like a Colossus, and we petty men walk under his huge legs and peep about to find ourselves dishonourable graves. The fault, dear Brutus, is in ourselves, that we are underlings. "Brutus" and "Caesar": what should be in that *Caesar*? Why should that name be sounded more than yours? Write them together, yours is as fair . . . weigh them, it is as heavy; conjure with them, Brutus will start a spirit as soon as Caesar!'

Again he compelled his friend's attention, refusing to let him turn away. 'When was there a time, when Rome was not famed with more than with *one man*? When could they say, till now, that her wide walls encompassed but *one man*?'

Brutus gazed into Cassius' face, and then away again. He passed a hand across his eyes, wearily. 'I have some notion of what you would work me to,' he murmured. And then he seemed to gather strength, and spoke with emphasis. 'What you have said, I will consider. What you have to say I will with patience hear, and find a time to hear and answer such high things.'

He paused. Caesar was returning, drawing the joyful multitudes with him. The celebration games were over.

But on the dictator's face there was the hot burn of anger . . . and his wife Calpurnia looked pale. It seemed that Mark Antony had run into the great market place to end the race, and there had offered a king's crown to Caesar!

Caesar had pushed the crown away. A second time Mark Antony had offered it, and then a third. Three times had Caesar rejected it, firmly, and each time the crowd had cheered . . .

But Caesar had been angered by the people's glee that he refused the crown, for in his heart he wanted to be king. The heat and crush and noise of people pressing close had suddenly sickened him, and his old illness rose . . . There, before them all, in the great market-place, during the celebrations of his triumph, he had plunged into an epileptic fit and fallen, foaming-mouthed, onto the ground.

Returning now along the street, he had recovered. But he saw Cassius was watching him. For a moment he returned the steady stare, and then he spoke quickly, privately to Mark Antony by his side. 'That Cassius has a lean and hungry look; he thinks too much, such men are dangerous.'

'Fear him not, Caesar,' Mark Antony was confident. 'He's not dangerous. He is a noble Roman, and well disposed.'

Caesar shook his head. 'Such men as he be never at heart's ease while they behold a greater than themselves, and therefore they are very dangerous.' But now he shook the lingering gloom away, 'I rather tell you what is to be feared, than what *I* fear,' he asserted, 'for always I am Caesar!'

The night was wild, the sky blue-shot with lightning flame and thunder hammered like a war in heaven. The people talked of weird, unearthly happenings: a slave who's hand burned like twenty torches while his skin remained untouched, lions lurking around the Capitol . . .

Under cover of this monstrous night, Cassius gathered men to work a bloody and most terrible task: other senators who feared, loathed, or resented Caesar, and wished his power removed.

And under cover of this fuming night there were papers, forged by Cassius, thrown in at Brutus' window. All claimed to have been written by respected citizens. All spoke of the great faith Rome's people had in Brutus and their fear that Caesar aimed to be crowned as king. There were other letters pasted on the statue of Brutus' famous ancestor, Lucius Brutus, a hero who had rid Rome of its last king, the tyrant Tarquin. So, skilfully, did Cassius take Brutus' sense of honour, his love of Rome and hatred of all tyranny, and fashion them into a net to bind him into their conspiracy.

Brutus twisted in the snare. Since Cassius had first whet him against Caesar, he had not slept. Since that moment on the feastday of the first of March to this, the Ides of March, for all those fifteen long days, his inner struggle had not ceased. Was there any other way to stop the dictator's ruthless climb to absolute power? His mind could show him none. Caesar wanted to be crowned. Once beneath that crown, how might he change, how might he use his power *against* the liberty of Rome and all her people? How might that man, feeling his unchallenged strength, lose all pity for his fellow men and become a tyrant?

Brutus knew no reason to suspect Caesar *would* abuse his power: and he had no personal cause to hate this man. On the contrary he loved and most respected him. But what might he *become*, climbing the ladder upwards? That was the question. And what must be done to prevent the rot?

'It must be by his death.' The words, once out, were no more comfortable than when they lurked unsaid below the surface of his mind. 'Think of him as a serpent's egg which, hatched, would, as his kind, grow mischievous, and let's kill him in his shell.' Still he wrestled with the thought. 'Between the acting of a dreadful thing and the first movement, all the interim is like a hideous dream . . .'

'Sir, Cassius is at the door, and he desires to see you,' his servant broke through Brutus' thoughts with difficulty.

'Is he alone?'

'No, sir, there are more with him. Their hats are plucked about their ears and half their faces buried in their cloaks.'

So they had come to him: in the dead of night, the conspiracy, the faction against Caesar, cloaked in fear against discovery . . .

They entered, Cassius, and six others. Only Cassius showed openly who he was. The others huddled, hidden.

'Do I know these men that come along with you?' demanded Brutus.

'Yes, every man of them,' Cassius assured him, 'and all men here honour you and wish that you had that opinion of your honour which every noble Roman has of you.' And swiftly Cassius drew Brutus off, to lay their plan before him and bind the final threads to hold him: a call once again on his nobility and honour, to urge him out of the mire of self-debate and into the urgency of action.

Brutus made up his mind. 'Give me your hands all over, one by one,' he said suddenly. No oaths to bind them to their task, he urged, only their honesty and honour to keep them firm . . . and so he shook their hands. Trebonius, Decius, Casca, Cinna, Cimber, every one a fellow senator.

Cassius interrupted. 'I think it is not sensible that Mark Antony, so well beloved of Caesar, should outlive Caesar: we shall find him a shrewd contriver. Let Antony and Caesar fall together.'

Brutus stopped him short. 'Our course will seem too bloody, Cassius, to cut the head off and then hack the limbs, like wrath in death and envy afterwards. Antony is but a limb of Caesar: let us be sacrificers, not butchers.' He stared beyond the hideous deed they planned towards the glorious future that would follow. 'We all stand up against the spirit of Caesar, and in the spirit of men there is no blood.' If only they could reach Caesar's spirit and not dismember Caesar! But alas, Caesar must bleed for it!

He turned with fierce conviction towards the other men. 'Gentle friends, let's kill him boldly, but not wrathfully; let's carve him as a dish fit for the gods, not hew him as a carcass fit for hounds . . . and for Mark Antony, think not of him. He can do no more than Caesar's arm when Caesar's head is off.'

'Yet I fear him,' insisted Cassius, 'for the great love he bears to Caesar . . .'

Brutus would hear no more of killing Antony. Morning light already warmed the sky, and soon this day to end the growing tyranny of Caesar would begin. It must be marred by no more than what they *had* to do.

Cassius obeyed. 'Friends, disperse yourselves: but all remember what you said and show yourselves true Romans!'

Brutus watched them go. Now the choice was made. Now, on this Ides of March, the inner war could stop. He had decided, and he had decided for the good of Rome and all its people.

Caesar had not slept that night: neither the ominous boom of thunder nor Calpurnia, his wife, had let him rest. Three times she had cried out in her sleep, 'Help! They murder Caesar!' for she had dreamed she saw his statue running blood, and many lusty Romans bathed their hands in it, smiling . . . She begged him not to leave the safety of his house today to go to the senate.

'The things that threatened me never looked but on my back; when they shall see the face of Caesar, they are vanished!' Caesar dismissed her fears. Nor would he let her talk of grisly sights seen by the night watchmen, or of the hideous shrieks like groans of dying men in battle which had filled the darkness of the turbulent night.

'Danger knows full well that Caesar is more dangerous than he: we are two lions born in one day, and I the elder and more terrible. Caesar *shall* go forth today,' Caesar told Calpurnia.

'Do not,' Calpurnia begged on her knees. 'Call it my fear that keeps you in the house, and not your own. We'll send Mark Antony to the senate-house; and he shall say you are not well today.'

Caesar helped his wife up. As certainly as he had said a moment ago that he *would* go, he now said, 'For you, I will stay at home.'

But the conspirators had come to fetch him. They smiled at Caesar. They smiled at Calpurnia's fears, and told Caesar that her dream was not of horror, but a vision of good fortune: the statue spouting blood in which so many smiling Romans bathed showed that from great Caesar Rome would suck reviving blood, and that great men would press for tokens of the mighty leader!

They said that on this very day the senate had decided to bestow a crown on him! If he sent word he would not come, they might then change their minds! They might think, if he hid himself, that Caesar was afraid!

Caesar changed his mind. 'How foolish do your fears seem now, Calpurnia! I am ashamed I did yield to them. Give me my robe, for I will go. Good friends,' he urged the men who planned his death, 'go in and taste some wine with me; and we, like friends, will straightway go together.'

Caesar had reached the entrance to the senate-house. Around the steps clustered eager senators and on all sides men pressed forward with petitions and requests, with urgent cries for the dictator's attention to their pleas.

Among them stood the old man who had warned against the Ides of March.

Caesar saw him, and stopped. 'The Ides of March have come,' he told him, with a smile.

'Aye, Caesar; but not gone,' the voice shrilled above the tumult, and then was lost.

'Hail Caesar! Read this paper,' instantly another voice was raised, but in a moment it was pushed aside by other suitors for the dictator's ear. Urgently the first man persisted, 'Caesar, read mine first: for mine is a suit that touches Caesar nearer; read it instantly!'

'What touches me shall be last served,' said Caesar, generous in his self-denial. 'What, is the fellow mad?' he asked, as again the man pushed forward yelling, 'Delay not, read it instantly.' And with an irritated gesture of denial, he began to climb the stairs.

Thus did Julius Caesar push aside the last remaining hand of help, for on the paper in that hand were held the names of the conspirators and details of their plot against his life.

Now all pressed more noisily after him, waving petitions and yelling above their neighbours' pleas.

Behind the thronging crowd, Cassius and Brutus mounted the stairs. At Cassius' elbow another senator appeared. He leaned towards them, low-voiced and secretive, 'I wish your enterprise today might thrive,' and then he advanced smiling, towards Caesar. In consternation fast becoming panic, they stared after him. Their plot already known and *Caesar* about to hear of it!

'Brutus, what shall be done?' hissed Cassius. 'If this be known, Cassius or Caesar never shall turn back, for I will slay myself!'

'Cassius, be constant,' Brutus calmed him. 'They speak not of our purpose, for look, he smiles, and Caesar does not change.'

The moment of blank terror gone, Cassius breathed deep. Now nothing stood between them and their deadly task. Caesar was hemmed in by senators all talking urgently. Already their fellow conspirator Trebonius was drawing Mark Antony aside . . .

Last instructions whispered: 'Casca, you are the first that rears your hand,' Cassius reminded him. Metullus Cimber pushed his way to Caesar and presented his petition: a pardon for his banished brother Publius Cimber. Loudly Caesar rejected it. Brutus pressed closer and repeated the request. Still Caesar was adamant: no pardon. Cassius fell to his knees to add his voice.

Caesar, finding his decision still questioned, now grew angry. 'I could be well moved, if I were like you,' his tones boomed out above them. 'But I am constant as the northern star. The skies are painted with unnumbered sparks; they are all fire and every one does shine, but there's but one in all that holds his place: so it is in the world; men are flesh and blood, and apprehensive: yet I do know but one that unassailable holds on his rank, unshaked of motion: and that I am he. I was constant Cimber should be banished, and constant do remain to keep him so!'

'Oh Caesar . . .' came Cinna's cry.

'Begone!' said Caesar, still unmoved.

'Great Caesar . . .' pleaded Decius.

'Does not even Brutus kneel to no avail?' said Caesar angrily.

'Speak, hands, for me!' came Casca's rallying cry. And then the blow.

Caesar staggered beneath the dagger's stab and lifted up his hands to feel, in disbelief. Then a second, third, fourth, fifth . . . each chopped his sword or dagger down again, again, again. And then the last.

Caesar raised his eyes in pain and shock to Brutus' face. Brutus stabbed.

'And you, Brutus,' Caesar moaned, and fell to the ground, writhed, and lay still.

It was done. Gored and bleeding at the base of Pompey's statue lay the mighty Caesar, dead.

Silence. The white chill of shock and panic freezing limbs and brains, the senate stood and stared. So fast it had all happened that even those who understood had only risen from their seats, before the final blow was cast.

Cinna was the first to break the spell. 'Liberty! Freedom!' he yelled. 'Tyranny is dead! Run out, proclaim it, cry it about the streets!'

Swiftly Brutus intervened, lest fear should push them out into the streets and turn this triumph to a spreading panic. 'People, senators, be not afraid,' he urged. 'Ambition's debt is paid.' He flung his arms out wide to encompass his fellow conspirators. 'Stoop, Romans, stoop, and let us bathe our hands in Caesar's blood up to the elbows, and besmear our swords: then walk we forth, even to the market-place, and waving our red weapons over our heads, let's all cry, 'Peace, freedom and liberty!'

'Stoop, then, and wash,' cried Cassius exultantly. 'How many ages after this shall this our lofty scene be acted over in states unborn and accents yet unknown! And so often shall we be called the men that gave our country liberty!'

They bent over the bloody shape that lay before them on the ground in tremulous celebration of the sacrifice, each man's head filled with the deed that he had done and the future they believed it bought for them.

Behind them, silent, a new figure entered the senate house, and stood regarding them.

Brutus straightened up, and turned.

It was Mark Antony's servant. He gazed at the bleeding body on the ground. He raised his eyes and spoke to Brutus.

'Thus did my master bid me say,' he said, quietly. 'Brutus is noble, wise, valiant and honest: Caesar was mighty, bold, royal, and loving. Say I love Brutus, and I honour him; say I feared Caesar, honoured and loved him.' Now Antony's servant raised his voice steadily. 'If Brutus will promise that Antony may safely come to him and have explained how Caesar has deserved to lie in death, Mark Antony shall not love Caesar dead as well as Brutus living, but will follow the fortunes and affairs of noble Brutus through the hazards of this untrod state with all true faith. So says my master Antony.'

'Your master is a wise and valiant Roman,' Brutus' voice warmed with relief. 'I never thought him worse. Tell him to come to this place. He shall be satisfied, and, by my honour, depart untouched.'

With a nod, the servant left. 'I know that we shall have Antony as a friend,' said Brutus. Would not all true Romans only need to hear their reasons for this deed, to share its triumph, to revel in Rome's new-found liberty?

Cassius shook his head. 'I wish we may have Antony a friend: but yet I have a mind that fears him much . . .'

And Antony was already among them. He entered fast, and seemed to have no eyes for any but the bloody bundle on the ground. He stood in silence over it, his back to them, speaking in low private tones, 'Oh mighty Caesar! Are all your conquests, glories, triumphs shrunk to this little measure?' There was a long silence and impatiently Cassius moved towards him. Brutus caught his arm and motioned him to stay.

Now Mark Antony turned, his face composed and quiet. 'I know not, gentlemen, what you intend, who else must bleed, who else is rank: if I myself, there is no hour so fit as Caesar's death hour, nor no instrument of half that worth as those your swords, made rich with the most noble blood of all this world. Now, while your purpled hands do reek and smoke, fulfil your pleasure . . .'

'Antony,' interrupted Brutus, 'beg not your death of us. Though now we must appear bloody and cruel, our hearts you do not see. They are pitiful; and pity for the general wrong of Rome. To you our swords have leaden points, Mark Antony. Our arms and hearts do receive you in with all kind love, good thoughts and reverence. Only be patient till we have calmed the multitude, beside themselves with fear. And then we will explain the cause, why I, that did love Caesar when I struck him, have done this.'

Antony surveyed them quietly, moving his eyes across each face and bloody hand, though what was in the thoughts passing behind those eyes, no one could tell.

'I do not doubt your wisdom,' he said to them.

'Our reasons are so full of good regard, that were you, Antony, the son of Caesar, you should be satisfied,' Brutus assured him eagerly.

'That's all I seek,' Mark Antony affirmed, 'and ask that I may produce his body in the market-place, and in the pulpit, as a friend, speak at his funeral.'

'You shall, Mark Antony,' cried Brutus, generous in his renewed belief in Antony's goodwill to them.

'Brutus, a word with you,' said Cassius sharply, drawing Brutus to one side. 'You know not what you do,' he hissed. 'Do not consent that Antony speak at his funeral! Do you know how much the people may be moved by that which he will utter?'

Brutus would hear no argument: now that the deed was done, he was exultant in his confidence that all would understand it was a sacrifice for Rome. *He* would speak first in the pulpit and give their reasons, and only after, would Antony address the crowd. The citizens would see that Antony spoke only with Brutus' permission and that the men who had killed Caesar wished him to have all honourable rites and ceremonies in death. Brutus' confidence bounded on: it would appear greatly to their credit to have won the loyalty of Caesar's friend and faithful ally, Mark Antony!

'I like it not,' repeated Cassius doggedly.

But already Brutus was giving these conditions to Mark Antony: he could in his funeral speech speak well of Caesar but may not utter a single word of ill about those who had killed him. And he must make it clear he spoke only by their permission.

'Be it so,' agreed Mark Antony. 'I do desire no more.'

'Prepare the body then, and follow us,' commanded Brutus, and out they went.

Antony was alone. The senate-house had emptied of conspirators and witnesses to their grisly deed. Only the crumpled body of dead Caesar stayed, his blood glistening across the base of Pompey's statue where he had fallen as he died, and Antony, who stood and looked at it.

It was a different Antony from he who spoke soft words of peace to Julius Caesar's killers. He felt the silence drop about the senate halls, and looked up, and on his face was carved a very different tale from that he told to Brutus.

He whispered now, and they were words only for the bleeding corpse before him, 'Oh pardon me, that I am meek and gentle with these butchers! You are the ruins of the noblest man that ever lived in the tide of times.' His voice cracked.

He dropped to his knees beside the body, and in one hand he gripped the shreds of robes, ripped bloody with every dagger's gash into the flesh of Caesar. 'Woe to the hands that shed this costly blood! Over your wounds now do I prophesy, a curse shall light upon the limbs of men; domestic fury and fierce civil strife shall harass all the parts of Italy, and Caesar's spirit, ranging for revenge shall with a monarch's voice cry "Havoc," and let slip the dogs of war!'

In the great central market-place the people waited, grimly restless. Rumours flew from mouth to mouth, half-truths gathered like buzzing bees, grew to monstrous certainties, and then were flung aside. Fear and mourning hung like a shroud about the square.

'We will be satisfied,' the cry went up, and became a chant that swelled and filled the anxious air with ominous mutiny. 'Let us be satisfied. Let us be satisfied.'

Boldly Brutus stepped among them. He raised his hand for silence. At all costs, the vast numbers of people pressing in the square must be divided and then calmed. He urged some to stay and listen to what he had to say, others to go with Cassius and hear his words.

The crowd parted, reformed to shouts and cries, as this or that citizen declared that he would hear Cassius or Brutus. 'And compare their reasons!' the shout was heard. It hung threatening above the square. Cassius, followed by a knot of yelling men, marched to another street.

Brutus mounted to the central pulpit. Below, the crowd heaved to and fro as some pushed closer, elbowing a path; the noise swelled and faded and then swelled again . . . and, suddenly, silence fell. All stared suspiciously at the man who had, they heard, killed mighty Caesar.

'Romans, countrymen!' Brutus raised his voice and sent it loud across the square. 'Hear me for my cause, and be silent that you may hear: believe me for my honour, and have respect for my honour, that you may believe: blame me in your wisdom, and awake your senses that you may better judge.' He paused and looked slowly round the assembled multitude. Already their sullen curiosity was giving way to something else . . .

'If there be any here,' cried Brutus, 'any dear friend of Caesar's, to him I say that Brutus' love for Caesar was no less than his! If then that friend demand why Brutus rose against Caesar, this is my answer: not that I loved Caesar less, but that I love Rome more!' He paused again. Every man and woman watched. Silence reigned. 'Would you rather Caesar were living, and die all slaves, than that Caesar were dead, and live all free men?'

Across the silence murmurs rippled: cautious voices of assent. One or two nodded openly: his point was taken.

To cement this hopeful mood, Brutus continued quickly, 'As Caesar loved me, I weep for him; as he was fortunate, I rejoice at it; as he was valiant, I honour him,' again he paused, to ensure absolute attention, 'but as he was *ambitious*, I slew him! There is tears for his love; joy for his fortune; honour for his valour; and *death* for his ambition!'

He leaned across the pulpit, staring hard into the faces of the crowd, 'Who is here so base that he would be a slave? If any, speak; for him have I offended. Who is here that would not be a Roman? If any, speak;

for him have I offended. Who is here so vile that will not love his country. If any, speak, for him have I offended.'

Each question rang its insistent rhythm across the square, and as each echo faded, the shaking heads and sympathetic murmurs grew, the rumbling mounting to a single triumphant answer, 'None, Brutus, none!'

Brutus gazed with misting eyes across the mass of Romans spread before him. How clearly, in their nobility, they understood what Brutus and his fellows had to do for liberty in Rome! And would not all right-minded people understand?

A drumbeat boomed across their heads. All turned. Into the square strode Mark Antony, with others, and between them Caesar's body. The murmurs died, stifled by the sight of Julius Caesar's death, so stark and unmistakable.

Sensing the people's shock, Brutus claimed their attention hastily. 'Here comes his body, mourned by Mark Antony: who, though he had no hand in his death, shall receive the benefit of his dying, a place in the commonwealth.' He lifted up his arms, to encompass all of them. *'As which of you shall not?'* He raised a hand again to ask for quiet. 'With this I depart; that, as I slew my best friend for the good of Rome, I shall have the same dagger for myself when it shall please my country to need my death.'

It was as though he had rung a bell to signal ecstasy. The crowd went wild. 'Live, Brutus! live, live!' the nearest cried. And farther off, 'Give him a statue with his ancestors!' And then rising above all else, 'Let him be Caesar!'

Brutus turned his head with sudden shock towards the anonymous cry: a new dictator to replace the old!

Already Mark Antony was mounting the pulpit. He reached the top and surveyed the crowd. 'For Brutus' sake, I am beholden to you,' he said cautiously.

'It were best he speak no harm of Brutus here!' came a mutter from the crowd.

'This Caesar was a tyrant,' came another. 'We are blest that Rome is rid of him.'

Mark Antony was beginning. 'Friends, Romans, countrymen, lend me your ears.' The murmuring of the crowd fell silent. 'I come to bury Caesar, not to praise him.' Heads nodded, approving this simplicity. To bury was fair; but not to praise a tyrant!

Antony continued. 'The evil that men do lives after them; the good is often interred with their bones: so let it be with Caesar.' He moved to the front edge of the pulpit, and looked down. All stood upon their toes to see. Below him lay the body, gory with its seeping wounds.

'The noble Brutus has told you Caesar was ambitious. If it were so, it was a grievous fault.' He paused again, and continued to gaze upon the corpse. 'And grievously has Caesar answered it.' It was as though the crowd had suddenly become a single watching eye, fastened like a gigantic bird of prey on Antony. 'Here, with the permission of Brutus and the rest, for Brutus is an honourable man . . .' the word lingered in the air, and seemed to pick up echoes, 'so are they all, all *honourable men* . . . I come to speak at Caesar's funeral. He was my friend, faithful and just to me: but Brutus says he was ambitious: and Brutus is an honourable man.'

For a moment it seemed that Antony had finished. Restless movement rippled across the ranks, gloomy with disappointment. But in a moment he began again. And Antony's voice was louder now. 'You all did see that on the feast day I three times presented him a kingly crown, which he three times refused: was this ambition?' More murmurs, quickly dying, lest Antony's next word be lost. 'Yet Brutus says he was ambitious, and sure *he* is an honourable man. I speak not to disprove what Brutus spoke, but here am I to speak what I do know! You did all love him once, not without cause: what cause withholds you then, to mourn for him?' Uneasily, the vast crowd shifted, teetering . . .

And like a cannon's boom, Mark Antony's voice blasted in their ears, 'Oh judgement! You are fled to brutish beasts, and men have lost their reason!' Trembling, he glared across the mass, his face grown white with anger. And then he seemed to shake himself, and spoke more quietly. 'Bear with me: my heart is in the coffin there with Caesar, and I must pause till it come back to me.'

Like a prowling animal now, the crowd writhed, surged a little forward, and from the silence, a muttering . . .

'I think there is much reason in his sayings,' said the citizen who had called Caesar a tyrant. 'Caesar has had great wrong.'

'I fear there will be a worse come in his place,' muttered another man.

'He would not take the crown; therefore it is certain he was not ambitious,' a third concluded.

Antony was speaking again. He surveyed them, measuring, 'Oh masters, if I were disposed to stir your hearts and minds to mutiny and rage, I should do Brutus wrong, and Cassius wrong, who, you all know, are *honourable* men . . .' He gathered pace, 'Here's a parchment with the seal of Caesar. It is his will. Let but the people hear this testament (which pardon me, I do not mean to read), and they would go and kiss dead Caesar's wounds and dip their napkins in his sacred blood, beg a hair of him for memory . . .'

'We'll hear the will,' the roar went up, 'read it, Mark Antony. The will! The will! we will hear Caesar's will!'

Antony stood listening to the swelling thunder of the crowd. In all his thinking Brutus had never understood this populace of Rome, this fickle, changing beast, moulded now by Antony into his own brutal weapon of revenge.

'Have patience, gentle friends,' he told them, 'It is not right you know how Caesar loved you. It will inflame you, it will make you mad: it is good you know not that you are his heirs; for if you should, oh, what should come of it!'

94

'Read the will!' they yelled.

'I fear,' said Antony, 'I wrong the honourable men whose daggers have stabbed Caesar . . .'

'They were traitors: honourable men!' they shrieked.

Antony descended from the pulpit into the crowd and gathered them to Caesar's body to read the will. But first, he lifted up the bloody robes for all to see: 'Look, in this place ran Cassius' dagger through: see what a rent the envious Casca made: through this the well-loved Brutus stabbed. This was the unkindest cut of all; for when the noble Caesar saw him stab, then burst his mighty heart . . . Oh, what a fall was there, my countrymen! Then I, and you, and all of us fell down, whilst bloody *treason* flourished over us.'

The final stone was cast. The multitudes seethed close about the savaged body, like a giant beast that sniffed and whimpered at a fallen friend . . .

And then with one gigantic cry, the fury broke. 'Revenge! Seek! Burn! Fire! Kill! Slay! Let not a traitor live! We'll burn Caesar's body in the holy place, and with the brands fire the traitors' houses!' And from the square they surged, hot with mutiny.

Alone beside the body, Antony breathed deep. Now was Caesar's spirit indeed alive. 'Now let it work. Mischief, you are afoot, take what course you will.' Now would the forces of rivalry for power unlocked by Caesar's death be savagely let loose!

Within twenty-four hours it was Antony, not Brutus, who controlled the city. Brutus and Cassius fled Rome. And into Rome came a powerful ally to Caesar's cause: his young grand-nephew and adopted son and heir, Octavius Caesar.

Rome plunged into bloody chaos, as Antony had prophesied. Citizens raged through the city looking for the murderers of Caesar. In their frenzy to search out their prey even a hapless poet by the name of Cinna, a close friend of Caesar's, was dragged away to death for no other reason than his name: it was the same as Cinna the traitor.

So began a vicious battle for control. In the vacuum left by Julius Caesar's death, Mark Antony, Octavius and a third, named Lepidus, seized power, ruling as triumvirs, dividing all the Roman Empire's territory in Europe, Africa and Asia between themselves. They drew up a list of those to die for treachery against Caesar, coldly bargaining life for life: their own brothers, cousins, nephews, all whom they judged guilty. A hundred senators to die.

In a world torn by the rivalries for power once held in check by Caesar's strength, the power of Antony and Octavius grew unchecked, while Brutus and Cassius, fled separately to exile, prepared for war against them.

At Sardis in Asia Minor, these one-time leaders of the conspiracy met again, each now leading the army legions they had gathered to their cause. Many months had passed since that distant Ides of March in Rome when Caesar fell. The bonds of warmth which tied them then had cooled: in the aftermath of the assassination and their hasty flight, and in this anxious mustering of arms for war, differences once hidden by their common purpose, now reared a menacing head. Each had grown suspicious of the other, and fear of their differences had sown a bitter discord.

How much more than minor quarrels reared their vicious jaws to mangle them! The world whose liberty Brutus had sought by killing Caesar was ripped by bitter quarrels between rival factions, while Octavius and Antony marched on to greater strength unchecked. Unwilling to look for the cause of the chaos in the tangled web of their conspiracy, or in the illusions of unquestioning honour and righteousness in which he had floated through the deed, Brutus found fault instead with Cassius: Cassius was betraying the nobility of motives for which they had sacrificed Caesar, sullying the honour of their cause with dubious methods for gathering men and money . . .

'Remember March, the Ides of March remember,' he told him angrily. 'Did not great Julius bleed for justice' sake? What villain touched his body, that did stab, and not for justice? What, shall one of us, that struck the foremost man of all this world but for supporting robbers, shall we now contaminate our fingers with base bribes, and sell the mighty space of our large honours for so much trash as may be grasped thus? I had rather be a dog, and bay the moon, than such a Roman!'

'Brutus, bay not me,' warned Cassius, incensed and hurt by Brutus' self-righteous accusations. 'I'll not endure it!'

'There is no terror, Cassius, in your threats,' coldly Brutus rejected Cassius' anger, 'for I am armed so strong in honesty that they pass me as the idle wind . . . I did send to you for certain sums of gold to pay my legions, which you denied me: for I can raise no money by vile means . . .'

'I denied you not,' protested Cassius angrily, 'he was but a fool that brought my answer back!' Fury mixed with a new despair, for suddenly he saw they teetered above a chasm which would split them for evermore. A dark world-weariness swept over him: 'Come, Antony, and young Octavius, come, revenge yourselves alone on Cassius, for Cassius is aweary of the world; hated by one he loves, checked like a slave, all his faults observed, set in a note-book, learned by heart to cast into my teeth!' He rounded sharply on Brutus, 'There is my dagger: strike, as you did at Caesar; for I know, when you did hate him worst, you loved him better than ever you loved Cassius!'

And suddenly they both saw the dark divide that yawned between them, and understood how close they came to plunging into it.

'Sheathe your dagger,' said Brutus quietly. Wearily he hauled at their years of trusted friendship to patch up their differences. At their peril they had ignored them when they planned the death of Caesar.

And Brutus was sicker at heart than Cassius could have guessed. He had just heard that his beloved wife, plunged deep in grief at his exile and the growing strength of Octavius with Mark Antony, had killed herself. He turned again toward his faith in Cassius and that vision of Rome's freedom which had spurred him on to what he'd done. What else was there to grasp at, as the war with Octavius and Mark Antony drew nearer? Already these two had reached Philippi in Greece.

Brutus was all for marching straight to fight. Cassius thought differently: better to exhaust the *enemy* with marching, while they, merely awaiting their arrival, would be well-prepared.

Brutus disagreed. It was with the same confidence that he had rejected killing Mark Antony and insisted on him speaking in the market-place at Caesar's funeral. If they allowed the enemy to march from Philippi, he argued, the enemy would gather people to their ranks in every land they passed through . . .

'Hear me, good brother,' protested Cassius desperately.

'Our legions are brimful, our cause is ripe,' insisted Brutus. 'The enemy increases every day. We, at the height, are ready to decline. There is a tide in the affairs of men, which, taken at the flood, leads on to fortune: omitted, all the voyage of their life is bound in shallows and in miseries. On such a full sea are we now afloat, and we must take the current when it serves, or lose our ventures.'

As before, Cassius gave in. 'Then, with your will, go on; we'll along ourselves, and meet them at Philippi.' There was no more to say.

In his tent, Brutus sought a kind of peace, listening to the strains of music played by a sleepy servant. He read awhile, or tried to, searching the words that clustered on the page for some hint of certainty in the grim time that loomed ahead, until the room grew strangely dark, and struggling to clear his aching eyes, he suddenly froze. A dark chill had crept into the tent, making the flickering candle gutter, and a shadow moved across the gloom, formless, growing stronger, swelling grotesquely into the shape of murdered Caesar.

'Why do you come?' breathed Brutus, shivering.

'To tell you that you shall see me at Philippi,' echoed the sombre voice of Caesar's ghost.

At Philippi the rival armies met: Cassius and Brutus facing young Octavius Caesar and Mark Antony.

'Words before blows: is it so, countrymen?' challenged Brutus.

'Not that we love words better, as you do,' retorted Octavius.

'Good words are better than bad strokes, Octavius,' Brutus replied.

'In your bad strokes, Brutus, you give good words,' said Antony. 'Witness the hole you made in Caesar's heart, crying "Long live! hail, Caesar!" Villains! You showed your teeth like apes, and fawned like hounds, and bowed like slaves, kissing Caesar's feet; whilst damned Casca, like a cur, behind struck Caesar in the neck!'

Octavius became impatient: hot words bandied were no alternative to the cold logic of brandished steel. 'Look,' he cried, 'I draw a sword against conspirators! When think you that the sword goes up again? Never, till Caesar's three and thirty wounds be well avenged; or till another Caesar has added slaughter to the sword of traitors!'

Compelled against his judgement to risk everything in this single battle here at Philippi, Cassius faltered before a sense of gathering doom. 'If we lose this battle,' he said to Brutus, 'then is this the very last time we shall speak together.'

Brutus looked long and hard into his friend's face, a forgotten gentleness between them warming the coldness of the future he too sensed. 'This same day must end that work the Ides of March began,' he murmured, 'and whether we shall meet again I know not.' He clasped Cassius' hand. 'Therefore our everlasting farewell take: for ever, and for ever, farewell, Cassius! If we do meet again, why, we shall smile. If not, why then, this parting was well made! Oh that a man might know the end of this day's business before it comes!'

That day did end the work the Ides of March began. On one flank Brutus pushed forward an attack on Octavius' force, and won. But he gave the signal to attack too early for Cassius' legions: forced into battle ill-prepared, they were swiftly overrun by Antony's troops.

Sinking ever deeper in despair, Cassius misread the signs of victory on Brutus' flank: watching his soldiers greeted eagerly by their victorious fellows, he thought that he had seen his troops vanquished by the enemy.

This was Cassius' day of birth: on this day he had entered the world, and suddenly he knew it was the day that he would leave it. Bowing before the overwhelming misery of the defeat he believed had overtaken them, he chose the traditional fate of Romans in defeat: death by his own hand. He gave his servant one final task: to guide the same sword that killed Julius Caesar into Cassius' breast.

Brutus, flushed with the excitement of his early victory against Octavius' force, received the news of Cassius death like the knell of doom. He rushed to the body of his friend. Now that same despair which had taken Cassius dropped like a shroud over Brutus. 'Oh Julius Caesar, you are mighty yet!' he cried. 'Your spirit walks abroad, and turns our swords into our own entrails! The last of all the Romans, fare well!' he mourned. 'Friends, I owe more tears to this dead man than you shall see me pay. I shall find time, Cassius,' he whispered, 'I shall find time.'

Before the day was out, Brutus tried their fortunes in a second fight. This time there was no victory: as the light of that ill-chosen day began to fade, the remnants of his defeated force clung with him and sought sanctuary in the creeping dark of night. And Brutus, who had sworn to Cassius that in defeat he would not look for death, now saw only this escape ahead of him.

'The ghost of Caesar has appeared to me two separate times by night: at Sardis once, and, this last night, here in Philippi fields: I know my hour is come,' he whispered.

'Not so, my lord,' his companions argued.

'I am sure it is,' he said again. 'Our enemies have beat us to the pit: it is more worthy to leap in ourselves, than wait until they push us. I shall have more glory by this losing day than Octavius and Mark Antony by this vile conquest shall attain,' he vowed and rallied his remaining strength of purpose, 'Brutus' tongue has almost ended his life's history: night hangs upon my eyes: my bones would rest, that have but laboured to attain this hour . . .'

And as he ran upon the sword held by his faithful servant, he gasped to the man whose death had haunted him each minute since that fateful Ides of March, 'Caesar, now be still,' and died.

Victorious Antony came upon the body of his enemy, and stood looking down at it. It was the final pinnacle of his success; and yet the taste of it was, in this moment, bitter.

'This was the noblest Roman of them all,' he mourned. 'All the

100

conspirators, save only he, did what they did in envy of great Caesar; he only, in general honest thought and common good to all, made one of them. His life was gentle, and the elements so mixed in him that Nature might stand up and say to all the world, "This was a man!'"

Octavius stood by his side. Now was the murder of Julius Caesar finally revenged; ahead lay only the fruits of victory. There was no power in the Roman world could challenge the might of Octavius and Mark Antony combined.

For the moment, at least, they stood together.

Antony & Cleopatra

The years had passed since Octavius Caesar and Mark Antony avenged the death of Julius Caesar on that bloody battlefield at Philippi. Now, with Lepidus, they ruled the Roman world. From its heart in Rome the arms of their power stretched to every corner of the ancient world.

But Mark Antony was not in Rome. Nor was he ranging the farflung reaches of the empire with the ordered legions of his army.

He was in Egypt. This mighty ruler of the ancient world had turned his back on all calls of duty from the stern halls of Rome, and in the languorous luxury of Alexandria he cavorted in love-games with a playful queen. He had become, so people said, the bellows and the fan to cool a gipsy's lust! Cleopatra, Queen of Egypt, and only Cleopatra, claimed the mind, hand and heart of Antony.

Wrapped in the ardour of Cleopatra's arms, Mark Antony was annoyed by the messengers from Rome who brought the breath of urgency, the severe demands of public duty like an icy blast across the idleness of love-locked days. They almost glowered at him with the disapproving brows of young Octavius Caesar himself!

'Nay, hear them, Antony,' teased Cleopatra, withdrawing amongst the perfumed fans of her attendants. Perhaps, she taunted, his abandoned wife, Fulvia, was angry. 'Or who knows if the scarce-bearded Caesar has not sent his powerful mandate to you: "Do this, or this: conquer that kingdom, give liberty to that. Perform it, or else we damn you!"'

'Let Rome in the River Tiber melt, and the wide arch of the ranged empire fall!' Antony dismissed the empire, Octavius, and all and clasped the laughing Cleopatra in his arms. 'Here is my space! The nobleness of life is to do thus,' he kissed her with the long, searching kiss of passion. 'Now, for the love of Love and her soft hours, let us not

disturb the time with harsh talk. There's not a minute of our lives
should stretch without some pleasure now. What sport tonight?' he
cried.

'Hear the ambassadors,' said Cleopatra, stemming the tide of words
with a kiss, for as he spoke she felt all the infinite certainties of his love
and knew no fears of losing him.

'Fie, wrangling queen,' he refused and caught her to him once again.
'No messenger but yours; and all alone tonight we'll wander through
the streets and note the qualities of people. Come my queen; last night
you did desire it.'

'Speak not to us!' he warned Octavius' messengers as he passed, and
a moment later he was lost to view, lost to the demanding eyes of Rome,
sinking again into the vast pleasure-garden of his love with Cleopatra.

It did not last. In the midst of that night's mirth Antony left the
festivities abruptly, and Cleopatra knew he thought of Rome.

She went in search of him. But when she saw him moving along the corridor with Rome's ambassador, she felt the impending threat of his departure drop like a chill shroud about her. Instantly she chose a punishment for his intruding thoughts of distant Rome.

'We will not look upon him: go with us,' she announced to her attendants, and swept out of sight.

Antony had consented, finally, to hear the news from Rome, and in an instant the grim rhythm of the world outside these walls gripped him like a vice: his wife, Fulvia, had gone to war against his brother, Lucius. Then, still discontented, she had joined with Lucius and together they'd made war on Octavius Caesar, had met defeat and been driven out of Italy.

Worse still, Labienus, a long-standing enemy of Rome, had with the army of the Parthians seized Asia from the Euphrates River, flourishing his conquering banner from Syria eastward to the coast of Asia Minor.

And Antony? Where was Antony, this all-powerful general of the Roman world? Antony saw the unspoken question in the ambassador's face, and suddenly Cleopatra's web of love dragged at him like a prison's chains. 'These strong Egyptian fetters I must break,' he breathed, 'or lose myself.'

There was more: another messenger had come, bringing the news that Fulvia was dead.

It brought no sorrow with it. Antony had long desired to be free of her: his heart had room only for Cleopatra. But thoughts of Rome again broke through the all-consuming image of his love. 'I must from this enchanting queen break off,' he told himself. 'Ten thousand harms, more than the ills I know, are hatched by my idleness.'

'I must with haste leave here,' he repeated his decision to his friend and fellow soldier, Enobarbus. 'I must be gone.'

'Cleopatra, catching but the least noise of this, dies instantly,' Enobarbus told him dryly. 'I have seen her die twenty times upon far poorer reasons!'

'She is cunning past man's thought,' smiled Antony with the confidence of one who already viewed the enchantments of the capricious queen across a widening distance.

'Her passions are made of nothing but the finest part of pure love,' Enobarbus nodded wryly. 'We cannot call her winds and waters sighs and tears: they are greater storms and tempests than almanacs can report.'

'Would I had never seen her!' said Antony, suddenly.

'Oh, sir,' Enobarbus shook his head. 'You had then left unseen a wonderful piece of work!'

'No more light answers,' Antony told him with an air of fresh decision. The call from Rome was ringing in his ears again: too many letters from too many friends begged his immediate return. From inside and out the empire was under threat and its security hung by the slenderest of threads: no less than civil war was looming. Eight years ago there had been civil war when Julius Caesar fought the rival general Pompey and defeated him. Now the youngest son of Pompey was riding inward on the tide of his dead father's fame, prepared to challenge for the rule of Rome itself. Already young Pompey commanded the empire of the sea, and his support on land was growing among those who had not thrived beneath the rule of Octavius, Antony and Lepidus.

'Let our officers have notice of what we intend,' Antony commanded Enobarbus. 'I shall break the cause of our urgency to the queen, and get her permission to depart . . .'

'Where is he?' Cleopatra was asking Charmian, her attendant. 'See where he is, who's with him, what he does,' she gave instructions to another. And then hastily she called him back. 'I did not send you,' she reminded him to play his part with care. 'If you find him sad, say I am dancing; if in mirth, report that I am sudden sick: quick, and return!' And seeing Antony approaching, she threw a hasty faint into Charmian's arms. 'Help me away, dear Charmian, I shall fall . . . Pray you, stand further from me,' she instructed Antony haughtily.

'What's the matter?' asked Antony in some bewilderment. He had come with news of Fulvia's death and reasons for his return to Rome, and already they were fleeing from his tongue.

'What says the married woman?' demanded Cleopatra, giving him no chance to say any of it, for she was balanced precariously between her terror that he might say he planned to go to Fulvia, and anger that he even dared to think of it.

'You may go,' she dismissed him sharply. 'Let her not say it is *I* that keeps you here. I have no power upon you. Hers you are!' She turned her back on him, 'Never was there a queen so mightily betrayed!'

'Cleopatra . . .' protested Antony.

'Why should I think you can be mine and true, who have been false to Fulvia?' she raged.

'Most sweet queen . . .' he tried again, and tried to show the letter in his hand.

'Bid farewell, and go,' she cried. 'When you begged to stay, then was the time for words: no going then. Eternity was in my lips and eyes, bliss in my brows' curve . . .'

'Hear me, queen,' yelled Antony, breaking from the tongue-tied silence wrought by her massive fury. And in a great rush of words, he told her: civil war in Italy; support for the young Pompey growing daily . . .

Last, he produced the reason which should remove all Cleopatra's terror at his return to Rome: his wife was dead.

'Can Fulvia die?' Cleopatra asked suspiciously. She eyed him, and in a moment a new torrent of accusations flooded over him: so this was how her own death would be greeted, with no sorrow, not a single tear!

'By the fire that quickens the Nile's slime, I go from here your soldier, servant; making peace or war as you decide,' he protested desperately, and buffeted by the storms of passion conjured in an instant by the queen, he sank back into silence, lost in the bewildering maze of Cleopatra's changes. Only when the storm was over, did he summon back his purpose from where it had taken refuge in the recesses of his mind.

'I'll leave you, lady,' he said, awkward in his determination.

She heard him, and she stopped. She stood looking at him. He turned away. In that instant she understood he truly meant to leave.

And in that moment, Cleopatra too was tongue-tied. 'Courteous lord, one word,' she began. 'Sir, you and I must part . . .' She faltered, 'but that's not it.' She began again. 'Sir, you and I have loved . . . but there's not it . . .' and she lapsed into silence, words vanishing before the understanding that the man she loved was leaving and she was powerless to stop him.

Finally, elaborately, she sighed. She murmured, 'Your honour calls you away, therefore be deaf to my unpitied folly, and all the gods go with you! Upon your sword sit laurel victory! And smooth success be strewed before your feet!'

Antony took her hand. Relief that she released him fought with misery that he was leaving with all the violence of the war to which he marched for Rome.

'Let us go,' he encouraged her, gently now. 'Come. Our separation will so fly that you, residing here, go with me, and I fleeing away, remain here with you . . .'

In Rome, Octavius looked for Antony's return impatiently and angrily. 'This is the news,' he told Lepidus with some disgust. 'He fishes, drinks, and wastes the lamps of night in revel. He hardly gave audience to our messengers or condescended to admit that he had partners!' Yet every hour the streets of Rome rang louder with news of Pompey's rising fortunes.

'Let Antony's shames quickly drive him to Rome,' muttered Caesar. He turned to Lepidus. 'It is time we two showed ourselves in the battlefield. To that end let us assemble immediate council: Pompey thrives in our idleness!'

In Alexandria Cleopatra plunged into a living death. 'Oh that I might sleep out this great gap of time my Antony is away,' she sighed to Charmian. 'Where do you think that he is now? Does he stand, or sit? Or does he walk? Or is he on a horse?' She clutched at messages from him, reliving each moment of their delivery with cries of admiration, tears of joy and wails of sorrow, while messengers from her to Antony flew thick after him.

And in Sicily, seat of his power, young Pompey's confidence was growing daily: already his fleets controlled the sea for he had the forces of two powerful pirates as his allies, and he contemplated with some pleasure the image of Mark Antony in Egypt, sodden in a field of feasts and drink that kept his brain fuming and his body tied in love with Cleopatra.

The news that Antony was *not* in Egypt but was expected every hour in Rome struck a note of unexpected fear in the bold young contender for power: Mark Antony's skills as a soldier and general were twice those of Octavius Caesar and Lepidus together. But, Pompey consoled himself, there was triumph also in the fact that *his* challenge to the triumvirs was enough to pluck Antony from Cleopatra's sumptuous arms.

Across the room, Octavius Caesar regarded Mark Antony with narrowed eyes. Mark Antony returned the measured look. Aging Lepidus watched both his fellow triumvirs nervously, pleading for gentle words and reconciling smiles to bind their alliance tight again, as it had been all those years ago, on Julius Caesar's death.

They had not met, these three pillars of the Roman world, since Antony had gone to Egypt, and since that time a forest of hidden differences had sprouted grievances, not least the wars by Antony's wife and brother against Octavius.

Antony dismissed them: these wars were not of his making, and in waging war on Caesar they waged war on the triumvirate, and so on Antony as well.

But other grievances were festering: with rising anger Caesar pointed out that in all Antony's months in Alexandria, he neglected to receive messengers, to answer calls for arms and aid . . .

These accusations Antony rejected too. The messengers, it appeared, had sprung upon him as he was feasting three kings and he was not his usual self! And the truth was that Fulvia had made wars in Italy only to entice him out of Egypt and away from Cleopatra . . .

With each of Antony's too-casual replies, Octavius Caesar glared more grimly. And to the watchful eyes of Enobarbus on one side and Caesar's close advisers on the other, there was no doubt that the sharp swords of civil war which threatened all of them had been forgotten in this poison of breeding disagreements.

Mecaenas, Caesar's adviser, stepped forward: the urgency of present need demanded them to put these quarrels aside.

Or, to put it another way, said Enobarbus, 'If you borrow one another's love for the instant, you may, when you hear no more words of Pompey, return it again: you shall have time to wrangle in when you have nothing else to do.'

'You are a soldier only: speak no more,' Antony frowned at him.

'I had almost forgot that truth should be silent,' retorted Enobarbus, unabashed.

'It cannot be that we shall remain in friendship, our conditions so differing in their acts,' said Caesar grimly. 'Yet, if I knew what hoop should hold us staunch, from edge to edge of the world I would pursue it.'

Agrippa, from Caesar's side, stepped to the fore. He had the hoop that Caesar looked for. Fulvia's death had made Antony a widower and free to marry, he pointed out. Let him take Octavius Caesar's sister, Octavia, as his wife, and so bind his political alliance with Caesar with a brother's determined loyalties!

There was a fascinated silence. All eyes turned expectantly on Antony, so newly sprung from the arms of Egypt's passionate queen, and known for his all-consuming love of her.

Antony regarded all of them, and measured the proposal. Far from Cleopatra's fervent call, this urgent cry for unity against the swords of civil war rang louder in his ears and he could not but acknowledge its insistent, warning rhythm.

'Let me have your hand,' he said to Octavius, suddenly making up his mind, 'and from this hour the heart of brothers govern our loves and sway our great designs!'

'There is my hand,' Octavius Caesar answered him. A cautious gleam of welcome to the pact softened, for a moment, the grim glitter of his eye. 'A sister I bequeath you, whom no brother did ever love so dearly: let her live to join our kingdoms and our hearts; and never fly off our loves again!'

'Happily, amen!' said Lepidus, bustling with relief.

And swiftly all retired, to despatch the marriage and the preparations for their war against young Pompey.

Behind their departing backs, Enobarbus shook his head, though whether with regret or disapproval or relief, or merely simple, plain amazement, no one could have told. And his old friends Mecaenas and Agrippa were more interested to hear him tell of Egypt's wonders than to digest further the wonders that had just passed here.

'Eight wild-boars roasted whole at breakfast, and but twelve persons there; is this true?' Mecaenas enquired in disbelief.

'This was but as a fly by an eagle,' Enobarbus assured him, 'we had much more monstrous matters of feast . . .'

'She is a most triumphant lady, if report be square to her,' Mecaenas said.

Enobarbus shook his head again, thinking of the absent queen whose presence reached across the world, even to this room. 'When she first met Mark Antony, she pursed up his heart, upon the river of Cyndus!' he laughed to think of it, and searched for words that could encompass the glory of that unforgotten moment. 'The barge she sat in, like a burnished throne, burned on the water: the poop was beaten gold, purple the sails, and so perfumed that the winds were love-sick with them; the oars were silver, which to the tune of flutes kept stroke . . .' and for the moment, even Enobarbus was transported by the memory. 'For her own person, it beggared all description: she did lie in her pavilion . . .'

His voice trailed off, remembering, and his listeners, understanding, said with wonder, 'Now Antony must leave her utterly!'

'Never.' Enobarbus tone was absolute. 'He will not. Age cannot wither her, nor custom stale her infinite variety . . .'

'If beauty, wisdom, modesty, can settle the heart of Antony, Octavia is a blessed prize to him,' Mecaenas assured Enobarbus.

Enobarbus only looked at them with some amusement. They did not know Cleopatra; nor, it seemed, did they know Antony.

In Rome Antony married Octavia, and promised to keep faith with her. But even as the echo of his words to her was fading, he felt the searching gaze of an old soothsayer, and turned to encounter the knowing eyes of one who saw far into the shadows of the future. On an impulse he hailed the man.

'Say to me,' he demanded, 'whose fortune shall rise higher, Caesar's or mine?'

'Caesar's,' came the stark reply.

Antony did not like it. The cold confidence of Caesar, that sharp efficiency, that grim belief in the demands of public duty, were all alien to Antony, and being so, he feared them.

'If you play with him at any game, you are sure to lose . . .' came the whisper of the soothsayer. 'Your spirit is all afraid to govern you when you are near him. But he away, it is noble.'

'Go,' said Antony brusquely, hating the truth of what the soothsayer said. Even the gamblers' dice seemed to obey Caesar!

'I will go to Egypt,' he said suddenly to himself, and it was more than a statement of intent. It was a confession, now: the calls to Roman duty were fading coldly beside the call to Cleopatra's love. 'I will go to Egypt. And though I make this marriage for my peace, in the east my pleasure lies . . .'

And so they went to meet young Pompey's challenge: Mark Antony, Octavius Caesar, and the aging Lepidus, their armies gathered and their powers as one.

In Alexandria Cleopatra smouldered for absent Antony, and filled up her days with memories of him, seizing on every messenger that came from him as though they brought life again to one who waned for wanting.

With the same ecstasy she greeted the messenger who brought a different news. She saw at once he nursed a miserable burden, and terror that Antony was dead shot through her, searing. But this denied, she paced frantically before the hapless messenger, filling the air with words to block the news she feared.

'Good madam, hear me,' he protested.

'Well, go to, I will,' she said, but moved immediately to stare with narrowed eyes at him searching for tell-tale signs, 'but there's no goodness in your face! I have a mind to strike you before you speak. Yet, if you say that Antony lives, is well, or friends with Caesar, I'll set you in a shower of gold and hail rich pearls upon you . . .'

'Madam he's well,' the messenger broke in.

'Well said,' said Cleopatra.

'And friends with Caesar,' he continued.

'You are an honest man,' she told him happily.

'But yet, madam . . .'

She swung round and glared. 'I do not like "but yet,"' she hissed. '"But yet" is a gaoler to bring forth some monstrous wrongdoer!'

Throwing all care to the winds, the messenger gulped out the news, 'Madam . . . he's married to Octavia!'

She stared whitely at him. She did not compehend. Then understanding shot through her with such fury that her hand flew up and struck the messenger across the face before he or anyone had understood the violence that tore through the shaking queen. 'Horrible villain!' she spat the words at him, 'I'll spurn your eyes like balls before me: you shall be whipped with wire, and stewed in brine, smarting in lingering pickle!'

'Gracious madam,' the messenger protested, trying to escape her flaying hands, 'I that do bring the news did not make the match!'

'Say it is not so,' she yelled. 'A province I will give you and make your fortunes proud!'

'He's married, madam,' the messenger repeated stoutly, and for his pains was forced to leap from the blade of a murderously drawn knife. 'Rogue, you have lived too long,' the hysterical queen was shrieking. 'Melt Egypt into Nile! and kindly creatures turn to serpents . . .' she sobbed, and fell on Charmian.

In a moment she had regained her calm and recalled the fleeing messenger to hear the news more coolly. It was no better for the retelling, and her coolness did not last. 'Let Antony for ever go,' she moaned to Charmian, and then 'let him not . . . Charmian, though he be painted one way like a monster, the other way's a god! Pity me, Charmian!' And then she raised herself to her full height, 'pity me, but do not speak to me!'

The sparring Roman parties met to talk before they went to war: on the one hand Pompey with his pirate allies and on the other the Roman triumvirs. And fronting power to power, they bargained for a settlement to tie up Pompey's discontented sword and buy peace. To Pompey the triumvirs offered the island realms of Sicily and Sardinia; in return, they asked that he would rid the seas of pirates and send shipments of grain to Rome.

Pompey, faced with a battle with the combined powers of all three triumvirs, found the peace bargain offered more attractive, for the moment.

And so it was agreed and the deal between them sealed. The order of the day became not bloodshed, butchery and death, but celebration, drink and food to hail this pact of peace. On Pompey's ship, anchored off the southern coast of Italy, these leaders of the Roman world and the would-be contender for their power, who might have been engaged in hacking off each other's limbs, gathered instead to shake each other's hands and embrace as friends.

'Sit! And some wine!' young Pompey cried. 'A health to Lepidus!'

The aging triumvir nodded with a blear-eyed pleasure, for he had drunk deep of wine along with his relief that war had blown from the horizon as swiftly as a puff of wind. He burped. 'I am not so well as I should be, but I'll never give up,' he announced with a solemn certainty denied by his slurring speech. 'Certainly, I have heard the Egyptian pyramises are very goodly things . . .' he continued stolidly, for the conversation when he last heard it had been of serpents and crocodiles in the Nile. 'What manner of thing is your crocodile?' he enquired of Antony, slipping sideways in his chair, and helped to a more stable stance by Enobarbus.

'It is shaped, sir, like itself,' declared Antony, and raised his cup in mirth to listening Octavius. 'It is as broad as it has breadth; it is just so high as it is, and moves with its own organs; it lives by that which nourishes it . . .'

'What colour is it of?' Lepidus pressed on doggedly.

'Of its own colour too,' nodded Antony, solemnly winking at his audience, 'and the tears of it are wet.'

'Will this description satisfy him?' wondered Caesar in amazement.

And while these all-important questions of the crocodiles and Lepidus were considered with sage concentration by the assembled company, Menas the pirate leaned towards young Pompey and whispered something in his ear.

He was roughly pushed away: Pompey had more important business to attend to in the drink still slopping in his cup. Menas grew fierce with insistence. Reluctantly, and angry with it, Pompey let himself be drawn from the scene of drunken celebration.

'Will you be lord of all the world?' Menas demanded in his ear.

'What do you say?' Pompey tried to swing his focus on the business so starkly placed before him, but viewed it through wine's shifting haze.

'Will you be lord of the whole world?' repeated Menas impatiently. 'I am the man that will give you all the world.' He turned, and nodded towards the triumvirs now slumped in raucous laughter round the table. 'These three world-sharers, these *competitors*, are in your ship: let me cut the cable; and when we are put off from shore, fall to their throats: all there is yours!'

Pompey reeled at the audacity of the proposal, and tasted it. The taste of wine and joviality was stronger. He flung his arm about the pirate's shoulder, 'Ah, this you should have done, and not have spoken of it! In me it is villainy; in you it would have been good service! Being done unknown, I should have found it afterwards well done; but must condemn it now.' He thumped his shoulder jovially, 'Leave it, and drink!' and he tugged the man towards the feasting table, raising his cup again to toast his new-made friends, 'This health to Lepidus!'

114

Thwarted Menas saw only that Pompey, who had given the dare to Caesar, now ducked the final choice for power in favour of a toast to sodden Lepidus, who sank finally beneath the tide of wine.

'There's a strong fellow, Menas,' Enobarbus said into his ear, pointing to the attendant who carried the unconscious triumvir away. 'He bears the third part of the world!'

'The third part, then, is drunk,' said Menas, bitterly.

'This is not yet an Alexandrian feast!' Pompey yelled.

'It ripens towards it,' said Antony, and thumped his cup across the table. 'Here is to Caesar!'

'I had rather fast for four days than drink so much in one,' groaned Caesar.

'Ha, my brave emperor,' Enobarbus applauded him. 'Shall we dance the Egyptian Bacchanals? All take hands,' he bellowed, as musicians struck up a rousing tune, and the pillars of the Roman world stomped in a drunken round carolling 'Cup us, till the world go round,' until the circle broke, and Caesar gasped to Antony, 'Good brother, let me request you off: our graver business frowns at this levity. Gentle lords, let's part. You see we have burnt our cheeks: strong Enobarbus is weaker than the wine, and my own tongue splits what it speaks!' He lurched a little, and reached out for Antony, whose constitution, strengthened by his Egyptian revels, was proving to have greater stamina.

'Take heed you fall not,' Enobarbus warned the lurching pair as they stepped from ship to boat to take them to the shore.

And thus the pact of peace was celebrated, and neither knew that on the spinning brain of drunken Pompey had rested, for that split second, the question of who would dominate the Roman world . . .

While Antony was thus engaged in drunken revelry in Italy, his army was in Syria under the command of Ventidius and there had put the warlike Parthians to flight and won still greater glory for their general's name.

In Rome again, the matter of young up-start Pompey settled, Caesar and Antony prepared to part and passed Octavia from a brother's to a husband's hand to bind their alliance firm.

And in Egypt Queen Cleopatra sent for the hapless messenger who had brought the news of Antony's new marriage. Her first terror at the loss of Antony grown calmer, her curiosity was restless. What was the Roman woman like, she who had stolen her love? 'Is she as tall as me?' she demanded.

'She is not, madam,' replied the messenger, cautiously.

'Did you hear her speak? Is she shrill-tongued or low?'

'She is low-voiced,' the answer came.

'Dull of tongue and dwarfish!' scorned Cleopatra, pleased. 'Guess at her years,' she demanded next.

'Madam, she was a widow . . .'

'Widow!' exclaimed Cleopatra. 'Charmian, listen!'

'And I do think she's thirty,' said the messenger, warming to his task. And so the vital exploration of her rival's charms went on, Cleopatra showering the messenger with promised gifts of gold for the pale description given. Antony could not possibly wish to stay with Octavia for long!

Antony had gone to Athens with Octavia. As Enobarbus had foretold, it was not long before the new-sealed friendship with her distant brother Caesar palled, and old angers bred anew between the rivals. Caesar spoke publicly in disparaging terms of Antony, and new wars began against Pompey . . .

Octavia, pawn in the game of power between her brother and her husband, struggled with the unequal role of peacemaker, pleading with Antony to put his grievances aside.

He would have none of it, though he conceded to Octavia that she could act as an ambassador between them and try her pleas for reconciliation. Yet in the same breath he vowed to begin his preparations for a war that would eclipse her brother.

'War between you two would be as if the world should cleave, and that slain men should solder up the rift,' she cried in misery.

But now the rivalries so precariously controlled burst from their bonds. Caesar and Lepidus made war on Pompey: no sooner was this done and Pompey dead, than Caesar accused Lepidus of treachery with Pompey and imprisoned the aging triumvir.

Antony and Caesar were poised, alone, against each other, and on their choices hung the course of peace, or the headlong plunge into the bloody chaos of new wars.

Events moved fast. With Octavia gone to plead for reconciliation with her brother, the last remaining bond with Rome was lost. Antony went to Cleopatra.

In Rome, with mounting fury, Caesar heard that Antony had abandoned Octavia, condemned Rome publicly, and bequeathed his empire to Cleopatra. Enthroned on chairs of gold on a silvered tribunal in the public market-place in Alexandria, beside Cleopatra, splendid in the robes of the Goddess Isis and with their children grouped at their feet, Antony had given her Egypt, lower Syria, Cyprus, Lydia: of all these he made her absolute queen. Their sons he had proclaimed the kings of kings, giving them Great Media, Parthia, Armenia, Syria, Cilicia and Phoenicia . . .

War loomed closer: Caesar made known in Rome that he would answer Antony's complaints, for Antony had accused Caesar of seizing Sicily from Pompey, yet not giving Antony his share, of not returning ships loaned to him for the war, of deposing Lepidus and taking his territories and revenues for himself.

Caesar sent his replies: he would grant Antony part of what he had conquered, but then he demanded equally his share of Armenia and Antony's other kingdoms in the east, which he was so busy giving away to Cleopatra . . .

Neither yielded. Antony assembled the kings of the earth for war: King Herod of Jewry, the kings of Libya, Cappadocia, Paphlagonia, Thracia, Arabia, Pont, Comagen, Mede and Lycaonia . . .

Enobarbus and Antony's other officers watched Cleopatra's involvement in the coming war with unease.

'Your presence must puzzle Antony, take from his heart, take from his brain, from his time, what should not then be spared,' Enobarbus told her sharply. 'It is said in Rome that your maids manage this war!'

'Sink Rome, and their tongues rot that speak against us!' Cleopatra cried. 'Speak not against it; I will not stay behind!' she warned Enobarbus.

Even as they argued, Antony appeared, exclaiming at the lightning movement of Caesar's fleet across the Ionian Sea towards them.

'Canidius,' he told his commanding officer, 'we will fight him by sea.'

'By sea! what else?' nodded Cleopatra.

'Why will my lord do so?' Canidius enquired, perturbed.

'Because he dares us to it,' said Antony, and smiled at Cleopatra.

'Your ships are not well manned,' protested Enobarbus. 'Your sailors are muledrivers, reapers, people swiftly pressed into this war; in Caesar's fleet are those that have often against Pompey fought: their ships are nimble, yours, heavy. No disgrace shall fall on you for refusing him at sea, being prepared for land!'

'By sea, by sea,' repeated Antony, deaf to all argument.

'Most worthy sir, you therein throw away the absolute soldiership you have by land, distract your army which consists of war-marked footsoldiers. You leave unused your skills . . .'

'I'll fight at sea,' said Antony impatiently.

'I have sixty sailing ships, Caesar has none better,' Cleopatra said.

And they would hear no further argument: Canidius was ordered to maintain the nineteen legions and twelve-thousand cavalry of Antony's mighty army unused on land until the battle fought by sea be over.

All the while, with dazzling speed, Caesar's fleet and army neared. On the plains of Macedonia, he gave his final orders to his commanding officer: 'Strike not by land; keep whole: provoke not battle till we have done at sea. Do not exceed the order, for our fortune lies upon this risk!'

At Actium off the coast of Macedonia, the rival fleets engaged, while on the land the two great armies held aloof. At the bloody peak of battle, while all around men threw their lives behind Mark Antony, Cleopatra's flagship hoisted sail and fled, her fleet of sixty flying in panic with her.

The thousands on the ships of Antony watched in disbelief: their mighty general, as if bound to the Egyptian queen by some invisible bond of self-destruction, turned and fled after her.

'We have kissed away kingdoms and provinces!' a soldier cried to Enobarbus. 'She once being turned, the noble ruin of her magic, Antony, claps on his sea-wing, and, like a doting duck flies after her: I never saw an action of such shame!'

It spelled, to all who saw it, the doom of Antony. Had Antony held steady, their fortunes on the sea might well have triumphed. Now, his forces began to crumble: six kings of Antony's eastern empire yielded at once to Caesar. Canidius, devastated by his general's desertion from the fight, prepared also to leave and join his legions to the victorious Octavius Caesar.

'I'll yet follow the wounded chance of Antony,' Enobarbus said, 'though my reason sits in the wind against me.'

Antony plunged into a despair so complete it seemed to him the land itself was ashamed to bear him. He urged his remaining followers to fly, to take his ship and gold and make their peace with Caesar.

'Where have you led me, Egypt?' he turned on Cleopatra bitterly.

'Oh my lord, my lord,' she moaned, 'forgive my fearful sails! I little thought you would have followed!'

'You knew too well my heart was to your rudder tied by the strings and you would tow me after: and that your call might from the bidding of the gods command me!' he cried.

'Oh, my pardon,' was all the queen could say, for the enormity of what had happened struck her almost dumb.

Antony buried his face in his hands. Wherever he looked he seemed to see the image of Octavius Caesar rise and look down with disdain upon the shattered greatness of Mark Antony, mocking this mighty general who could let that judgement which had once commanded half the world, now ride upon his passions into the heart of his own doom. 'Now I must to the young man send humble treaties, dodge and shuffle in the shifts of lowness,' Antony mourned. 'I, who with half the bulk of the world played as I pleased, making and marring fortunes.'

He reached suddenly for Cleopatra, hopelessness and anger so mingled in his love for her that even as he accused her, who knew he should accuse himself, his whole being longed for surrender to the smothering warmth of love with her. 'You did know how much you were my conqueror, and that my sword, made weak by my affection, would obey my love . . .' he whispered.

'Pardon, pardon,' she wept.

He raised her face to his. 'Fall not a tear,' he told her, gentle, again. 'Give me a kiss. Even this repays me . . .'

To victorious Caesar, encamped in Egypt, they sent their petitions: for Antony, permission to remain in Egypt, or if not granted, to live a private man in Athens. For Cleopatra, they begged to have the rule of Egypt back, for her and for her heirs.

Caesar had no ears for Antony's request. For Cleopatra there was a stark answer, starkly given. She could have her wishes, on condition that she drove Antony from Egypt or killed him there.

'To the boy Caesar send this grizzled head, and he will fill your wishes to the brim,' Antony told her.

'That head, my lord?' faltered Cleopatra, struck dumb by the enormity of the demand.

There was no pause in the conqueror's assault upon her. Hard on the heels of the first, a second ambassador was sent to win her from Antony. Cleopatra, crushed by the vastness of her fall with Antony from queen of a gigantic empire to a beggar even for her life, finally saw the magnitude of their common ruin.

She eyed Caesar's ambassador cautiously, feeling her way in untried territory towards some way out of their predicament. 'Tell Octavius I am prompt to lay my crown at his feet, and there to kneel,' she said. 'Tell him, from his all-obeying breath I hear the doom of Egypt.'

Searching her words for some promise of the impending betrayal of Antony, the ambassador urged, 'It is your noblest course,' and with the boldness of a messenger sent by the conqueror of the world, he pressed his lips upon her hand.

Antony, coming suddenly upon his love in close and familiar conference with his enemy's ambassador, saw it with the burn of jealousy like fire, saw only betrayal, smelled the stench of a rottenness that seemed to swell from Cleopatra like the corruption of a spell she cast to bind his judgement to his passion. Savagely he turned on the ambassador, and had him dragged away for whipping till he ran with blood.

'You were half blasted before I knew you,' he raged at Cleopatra, 'a deceiver ever.'

'Is it come to this?' whispered Cleopatra, whose groping towards a path for her survival had nevertheless not yet encompassed the betrayal of her love.

'Alack,' cried Antony, emerging from his outraged bitterness into the chaos of a thousand shattering illusions, 'our moon is now eclipsed; and it portends alone the fall of Antony!'

But yet, again, before the hour was gone, she drew him to her, and Antony, his rage and jealousy now spent, grasped at her words of love as though they were the sap to renew his faltering limbs. He soared suddenly towards new energy. He would rally his remaining forces and throw their fates upon another try at Caesar!

'Do you hear, lady?' he cried to her, 'If from the field I shall return once more to kiss these lips, I will appear in blood: I and my sword will earn our place in history: there's hope in it yet! I'll set my teeth and send to darkness all that stop me! Come, let's have another gaudy night: call to me all my sad captains; fill our bowls once more! Let's mock the midnight bell!'

Only Enobarbus, litening, understood the finality of the impending doom. 'Now he'll outstare the lightning!' he said, with miserable disbelief. He shook his head. Now he knew that even he, who had withstood the massing failures of Antony's wild choices, even he, the most faithful of all followers, would leave Antony.

Antony rose higher on the crest of defiant confidence; in a kind of ecstasy, he prepared to fight by sea and land to reverse his fortunes.

Caesar prepared by land and sea to complete the final defeat of Antony and spoke of the nearing time of universal peace across the Roman world.

Enobarbus succumbed to his despair for Antony, and went to Caesar's camp. Yet now he loathed what he had done and writhed with the poison of his betrayal.

Antony, strapped in his warrior's armour by Cleopatra's hands, marched with spirits high towards the port where ranks of men armoured for war awaited him, and there he learned bitterly that Enobarbus had gone.

Yet the bitterness was not for Enobarbus; it was for himself: in his friend's betrayal, he understood those truths about himself which he refused to recognize. 'Oh, my fortunes have corrupted honest men!' he cried, and gave swift orders that Enobarbus treasure be sent after him, along with gentle greetings and farewells.

Enobarbus learned of his deserted general's generosity, and knew he could not fight against him. 'No,' he cried, 'I will go seek some ditch wherein to die!'

That day brought unforeseen success for Antony: 'We have beat Caesar to his camp,' he cried exultantly. 'Run on before and let the queen know of our actions! Tomorrow, before the sun shall see us, we'll spill the blood that has today escaped. I thank you all!' he hailed his followers . . .

In Caesar's camp, by night, the sentinels came upon the dying

Enobarbus, who in his misery fell with the name of Antony upon his lips.

The second day of battle dawned. 'Their preparation is today by sea,' said Antony. 'I wish they would fight in the fire or in the air; we'd fight there too! But this it is: order for sea is given!'

Again, as once before, Antony threw all into the fight by sea. Again, as once before, he lost all. Cleopatra's fleet surrendered to the enemy.

'Betrayed I am,' he cried, 'Oh this false soul of Egypt! This charm, whose eye called forth my wars, then called them home; has fast and loose beguiled me to the very heart of loss.'

Cleopatra shook before the onrush of his fury and his belief that she'd conspired with Caesar for his doom. In panic she took refuge from him in a monument, and in her desperation to regain a measure of his love, sent word that she had killed herself and died with Antony's name escaping from her lips.

In equal haste she despatched her attendant to find out how Antony might take her death, so as to know how she might plot her onward course.

'I made these wars for Egypt,' Antony was moaning, 'and the queen, whose heart I thought I had, for she had mine, she has packed cards with Caesar and false played my glory for an enemy's triumph.'

Into the mire of his despair came the false news of Cleopatra's death, richly embroidered by the lavish tongue of her attendant who told of how she'd gasped her last with Antony's loved name upon her lips.

'Dead, then?' he said, and trembled at it. Though a moment before he had raged for her death, he knew now that there was nothing more for him. The long day's task was over. No more to do but to unarm, to throw off his warrior's clothes in which, so many years ago he'd come to her, and in which, on this dark day, he had lost her.

'I will overtake you, Cleopatra,' he breathed to the queen who'd bound his heart and mind and soul even to this orgy of destruction. 'I will overtake you, and weep for my pardon. I come, my queen, stay for me; where souls do couch on flowers, we'll go hand in hand, and with our sprightly port make the ghosts gaze. . . .'

Desperately he begged his last and faithful follower, his page, to end the life of fallen Antony. The page, refusing to the last to look upon the ruin of his master, instead killed himself.

Antony was alone. He yearned to escape the abyss of loneliness and dishonour that bared its jaws to swallow him. There was no one to help, and in this final hour, only himself. He fell forward on his sword. But, as if in some grotesque mockery of this day's failure, he did not die.

He called the guards. They backed in horror from his writhing form, and would not give the final stroke.

'Most absolute lord,' a voice came through his agony, 'My mistress sent me to you.'

And then he knew. Cleopatra's final, fatal game with him to buy her life, had bought his death. In a sudden premonition that he would kill himself, she had sent her servant to reveal the truth to him, too late.

'Bear me, good friends,' he begged his guards, 'to where Cleopatra waits. It is the last service that I shall command you.'

Barricaded high up in the monument, Cleopatra saw the dying form of Antony, and all the ebb and flow of her passionate struggle to survive seemed to swell like darkness to smother her, and she was dying in it.

'Oh sun, burn the great sphere you move in!' she cried. 'Darkling

stand the varying shore of the world! Oh Antony, Antony, Antony! Help, Charmian, help, Iras,' she begged her attendants, 'help friends below, let's draw him up.'

'I am dying, Egypt, dying,' came Antony's hoarse whisper, as his bleeding body was hoisted to them in the monument. 'Oh quick, or I am gone.'

'Oh welcome, welcome!' she cried. She clasped his head and smothered it with kisses. 'Die, where you have lived: quicken with kissing!' She clung to him, all else but the memory of love eclipsed. 'Will you die,' she sobbed, feeling the life of Antony ebbing. 'Shall I abide in this dull world, which in your absence is no better than a sty?'

He struggled to persuade her to make peace with Caesar and save her life. But as the last breath faded from Mark Antony, the Queen of Egypt seemed to tremble, as though his life, flying, took with it the flame of hers and left only the embers. And suddenly her cry rose in a shrill wail of devastation above the darkness of the monument, 'Oh see, my women, the crown of the earth melts, and there is nothing left remarkable beneath the visiting moon!'

News of Antony's death reached Caesar fast, even with the sword with which he'd killed himself, brought as proof . . .

Caesar stared at the pitiful thing in silence. 'The breaking of so great a thing should make a greater crack,' he said at last. 'The death of Antony is not a single doom; in the name lay half the world.'

And now he thought of Cleopatra, whose presence as the vanquished Queen of Egypt in Rome would make his triumph from this conquest absolute. He gave orders that she should be captured from the monument and watched with care, so that she could commit no act of suicide which would defeat his final victory.

Cleopatra, knowing that he planned to show her in his triumph in Rome receded into dreams of glorious Antony as she remembered him, and waited only for her moment of escape.

Caesar came to see the queen whose love had fired his rival even to the brink of self-destruction. She kneeled low before the Emperor of the Roman world. She acknowledged his absolute mastery over all the territory that had once been hers to rule. She called out her treasurer to give evidence of her possessions, all, she claimed, nothing withheld from Caesar's eye.

Not so, the treasurer denied. She had withheld enough to purchase what she wanted . . .

She flinched before her treasurer's desertion to her will. It was the ultimate treachery, the blow that spelled the finality of her doom before the triumph of Octavius Caesar. Not even this much loyalty could she command, once fallen from her power. Now she heard Caesar's promise that he meant no harm to her, and nodded her acceptance of his absolute mastery.

Caesar left. 'Now, Charmian,' Cleopatra whispered. 'Show me, my women, like a queen: go fetch my best robes,' and dreamy with the memory, she murmured, 'I am again for Cydnus, to meet Mark Antony! Bring my crown and all . . .'

They prepared. Unsuspecting, the guard let in an old man carrying a basket, so he said, of figs. The basket placed before the dreaming queen, the old man left.

'Give me my robe, put on my crown,' Cleopatra spoke. 'I have immortal longings in me. Quickly, quickly, good Iras,' she urged her young attendant. 'I think I hear Antony call. I see him rouse himself to praise my noble act. I hear him mock the luck of Caesar. Husband!' she cried to Antony, 'I come!'

She reached into the basket at her feet. She lifted from beneath the leaves a writhing snake, a poisonous asp of the life-giving River Nile. 'Come,' she spoke caressingly to it, 'with your sharp teeth this knot of life at once untie . . .' She placed the creature to her breast and closed her eyes, and seemed to wander in a dream again. 'Peace, peace,' she chided Charmian, whose sobs broke through her dream of death. 'Peace! Do you not see my baby at my breast, that sucks the nurse asleep? As sweet as balm, as soft as air, as gentle,' she crooned to the instrument of her escape into the world where Antony awaited her.

And so they found her, glorious in her death as she had been in life when she had captured Antony upon the golden barge at Cydnus. At peace, she sat, as though no more than slumbering. At her feet lay Iras, choosing death beside her royal mistress, and Charmian, who in a loving trance arranged the royal crown with gentle care before she too crumbled to the ground and died. Around their bodies only the glistening trail of the poisonous asp bore witness to their choice . . .

Caesar knew then that Egypt's queen, in this her final act, defeated him. 'Take up her bed, and bear her women from the monument,' he

said, quietly. 'She shall be buried by her Antony: no grave upon the earth shall clip in it a pair so famous.' And even Octavius Caesar, emperor of the whole world, paused for that moment in his relentless march to power to bow his head before the pity of their story, as great as was the once-remembered glory of Mark Antony.